(IN THE NAME OF GOD)

Title:
Strategic Thinking with the focus on Business
(The Basic Concepts)

Strategic Thinking with the Focus on Business
Authored by Dr. Fereidoon Bidollahkhany
Published by Amazon Kindle Direct Publishing
Global distribution of academic books
September 2023

ISBN: 9798860812789

Publisher: Amazon Kindle Direct Publishing

Publisher's Address: P.O. Box 806, Seattle, WA 98108, USA

Publisher's Website: https://kdp.amazon.com

Table of Contents

Don't settle for anything less. Rise up and optimize your talents through strategic thinking and a big dream. your god should be your guide in all things.

(Beethoven)

PREFACE

The sphere of strategic management delves into the significance of individuals, their intellectual assets, and thought processes in the construction and execution of strategies, and their influence on strategic leadership . The importance of individuals role, along with their intellectual properties and ways of thinking, in the formulation and implementation of strategy, as well as in the strategic leadership process in strategic management confirmed by researches in the field of strategic management.(Hambrick, 2007; Finkelstein et al., 2009; Adair, 2010). Evidence shows that there is a definitive correlation between an individual's strategic thinking capabilities and the nature of corporate strategy, interactions with the business environment, and overall performance (Hambrick and Mason, 1984; Olson and Simerson, 2015).

Contrasted with strategic planning, strategic thinking is recognized as a personal, uncapped, instinctive, inventive, and synthetic cognitive process. In contrast, strategic planning tends to be more analytical, collaborative, meticulous, and sequential (Liedtka, 1998; Graetz, 2002). Notwithstanding, certain methodologies inspired by Ansoff's (1965) and Porter's (1980) ideologies also classify strategic thinking as analytical cognition.

To avert deterioration and maintain the progress of their operations, it is paramount for professionals to nurture their strategic thinking skills. Given the rapid pace at which the competitive environment of any organization can transform, it is crucial to stay alert to emerging trends and be ready to seize these new opportunities.

Why do some individuals manage to establish prosperous businesses starting from scratch, while others fail? What makes certain people capable of recognizing, comprehending, and evaluating shifts in trends and environmental conditions, while others struggle? The answer seems to lie in strategic thinking - a skill some people seem to have, and others do not. In the modern corporate world, strategic thinking stands as a critical competency that managers must possess. Companies grappling with complex issues are in dire need of managers equipped with this strategic mindset. In this highly competitive global scenario, the key to capturing a larger market share lies in fostering and honing strategic thinking.

At various organizational levels, strategic thinking revolves around identifying and nurturing distinct opportunities that add value to the organization. For public managers, one of their most critical responsibilities is to anticipate future scenarios. Success is more probable for those who have a clear understanding of their goals, the resources at their disposal, the potential challenges they might face, and a viable strategy. However, planning is a complex process. Often, the plans we craft may seem disconnected from reality, and many may lack clarity right from their inception. With ever-changing circumstances and unforeseen issues cropping up, even the most meticulously crafted plans may be rendered irrelevant and discarded.

This raises some essential questions: Can we fulfill our obligations without efficient planning? If not, how can we weave sound planning principles into the fabric of management? The answers to these queries might be found in the practice of 'strategic thinking.' Concepts such as 'strategic planning and management' and 'developing strategic directions' all exemplify 'strategic thinking.'

Implementing strategic thinking can elevate productivity, job satisfaction, reduce stress, and often lead to the achievement of set goals.

Gaining proficiency in strategic thinking can empower you to effectively plan against unforeseen events, make smarter choices, and outwit your competitors with an improved sense of confidence and ease.

Incorporating strategic thinking into your everyday work and life routines enhances your ability to predict, foresee, and leverage opportunities, and manage resources efficiently.

With Strategic Thinking training, you receive a comprehensive and straightforward guide to the skills, tactics, techniques, tools, and case studies, all designed to augment your capabilities.

The competence to think strategically is increasingly vital for managers across various levels within organizations.

It aids in fostering innovative thoughts and creativity in your personal matters and ensures successful execution of your professional tasks.

Broadly speaking, strategic thinking is built on the fundamental ability to strategize. Not everyone, particularly those at the early stages of their career, has the opportunity to participate in strategic planning. However, everyone can develop strategic thinking skills. Thinking strategically can provide a competitive edge for an organization, team, or individual. Business professionals often believe they possess a strategic mindset but fail to comprehend and implement true strategy.

This training equips individuals with strategic thinking skills, enabling them to make informed decisions in their dynamic work environments.

This understanding helps in making effective decisions that yield long-term results. In pursuit of this educational goal, two books have been prepared catering to two levels: Basic and Supplementary. Currently, the Basic level book is at your disposal.

- By exploring this book, you will be able to:

    - Grasp the principles of thinking and strategic thinking and their related expressions.

    - Discern the difference between systematic thinking and strategic thinking.

    - Master the skills, techniques, and types of strategic thinking.

    - Understand how to enhance strategic thinking skills through conceptual questions for a deeper comprehension of the concepts.

Chapter 1: Thinking

Preface:

First, to better understand the content, I examined the book's key terms using various terminology sources as follows:

✎ **Thinking**

The word **"thinking"** means:

."The process of forming an opinion or idea about something, or the opinions or ideas formed by this process".(Cambridge Academic Content Dictionary,2023)

. The process of using your mind to understand matters, make judgments, and solve problems.

. The action of using one's mind to produce thoughts, opinions, and judgments. (Merriam Webster,2023)

. The activity of using your brain by considering a problem or possibility or creating an idea. (Collins,2023)

.Thinking is the cognitive process, the use of everything from long-term memory to come to an end or solution to the problem.

.The word think as the general word means to exercise mental faculties to form ideas which arrive at conclusions. (Webster's New World Dictionary,1988)

. Able to think intelligently about complicated things. (Britannica Dictionary definition of thinking,2023)

✎ Elements of Thought

Thinking effectively utilizes a variety of tools, such as mental images, concepts, and propositions. Here these elements are briefly described:

- Mental Images:

Research indicates that mental rehearsal can stimulate the brain structure, improving performance. Thus, mental images aid in planning actions based on information stored in our memory, thereby enhancing the results of a particular task effectively.

- Concepts:

Concepts represent mental constructs of a set of objects, people, events, or entities that bear common characteristics. For example, 'animals', 'birds', and 'individuals' are concepts of living beings. 'Blue', 'green', and 'yellow' are color concepts. Concepts facilitate cognitive efficiency and simplify communication. They allow us to categorize complex phenomena into simpler, more comprehensible, and applicable groups, assisting in problem-solving.

- Propositions:

Thinking incorporates languages, percepts, and symbols to imbue meaning into the cognitive process. Propositions articulate the mental manipulation of these cognitive skills (languages, mental images, concepts) to establish meaningful connections with our thoughts. Propositions shape mental models, guiding our knowledge structures related to objects, places, and events in our surroundings. An inaccurate model can result in errors in thinking and lack of action. For instance, the sentence "I like you" suggests a close relationship between two friends. If your mental model about that friend is flawed, you may harbor negative thoughts about him/her. Propositions create connections among our cognitive processes.

Thinking skills

Thinking skills are cognitive actions or steps taken to employ them to solve problems, make diverse decisions, formulate questions, design plans, organize, and generate information. These abilities are inherent in everyone, but their effective application varies among individuals. The development of effective thinking skills is a process that unfolds over time. We utilize these skills when we are confronted with problems, making decisions, organizing events, or assimilating information. Thinking skills equip us to process information, recall facts, and apply knowledge in various situations.

Thinking skills constitute the mental exercises employed to process information, establish connections, make decisions, and concoct novel ideas. We employ these skills when attempting to comprehend experiences, solve issues, make decisions, pose questions, devise plans, or organize data.

Thinking skills represent the cognitive activities we apply to process information, create connections, make decisions, and formulate innovative ideas. The most basic thinking skills encompass learning and recalling facts.

Central thinking skills encompass the ability to focus, organize, analyze, evaluate, generate inferences, gather, compile, and connect.

There are three categories of thinking skills:

"Analytical, critical, and creative thinking skills."

Analytical thinking skills entail the capability to detect patterns and relationships between ideas and events. Critical thinking skills denote your proficiency in understanding and resolving problems based on all accessible information and facts. Creative thinking skills correspond to your capacity to think beyond conventional limits and generate innovative ideas.

Thinking Types

Here are some of the most frequently utilized thinking styles:

1. Divergent Thinking:

This thinking style involves generating a wide range of potential solutions to a given problem.

Divergent thinking is often considered the most creative thinking style. There are no boundaries to the extent or nature of your thoughts. It is the birthplace of innovation, trendsetting, and transformational ideas.

The Four Pillars of Divergent Thinking are:

- Defer Judgment:
  During a divergent thinking exercise, every idea that surfaces is valuable due to the effort and time invested in its creation. Therefore, avoid judging any ideas at any stage. The aim is to create a comfortable space for participants to brainstorm freely, as judgment can halt the creative process.
- Gather All Ideas:
  Encourage participants to generate a multitude of ideas. These ideas can be brief, often only one or two words. In divergent thinking, an idea doesn't have to be a fully formed sentence or solution; those emerge later. Collect all ideas on sticky notes or digital whiteboard notes; everything has potential value.

- Create Connections:
  Generate interlinked ideas from all the notes. Establish connections through words, categories, emotions, and outcomes. As the facilitator, it's your job to identify connections, so don't limit the experience and the creation of more probabilities.
- Create new ideas:
  Combine concepts in ways you wouldn't typically consider. Let fresh ideas stem from these connections. Innovations flourish in an environment that encourages free ideation and unrestricted thought processes. Strive for ideas that evoke surprise and inspiration.

2. Convergent Thinking:

This thinking style involves narrowing down multiple possibilities to find a single, best answer to a problem. Convergent thinking is essentially the opposite of divergent thinking. While divergent thinking generates a wide array of ideas and solutions, convergent thinking utilizes logic to consolidate these ideas and shape them into feasible, concrete solutions.

Tips:

It's crucial to understand that no thinking style is superior or more important than others. Each has its specific uses and advantages at different stages of problem-solving. Divergent and convergent thinking often work in cycles - you start with divergent thinking to generate an array of ideas, and then use convergent thinking to refine these ideas into actionable solutions. Utilize them in harmony as complementary techniques.

3. Critical Thinking:

Critical thinking is the mental process of actively and skillfully conceptualizing, applying, analyzing, synthesizing, and evaluating information to reach an answer or conclusion. It's a way of thinking about whatever is occupying your mind at the moment so that you can reach the best possible outcome.

Critical thinking involves the capacity to analyze information objectively and make reasoned judgments. It's a component of emotional intelligence. Those with critical thinking skills can think clearly and rationally when situations demand it, enhancing their problem-solving and decision-making effectiveness. It allows individuals to delve beneath the surface-level understanding, analyze the logical connections between ideas or concepts, and extract valuable insights.

Critical thinking skills differ from creative thinking skills. While creative thinking is the generation of new, innovative ideas, critical thinking involves careful and logical analysis of given information.

Key skills needed for critical thinking include observation, analysis, interpretation, reflection, evaluation, inference, explanation, problem-solving, and decision-making. More specifically, we need to be able to:

- Think about a topic or issue in an objective and critical manner.
- Identify different arguments related to a particular issue.
- Evaluate a point of view for its strength or validity.
- Recognize weaknesses or negative points in the evidence or argument.
- Discern potential implications behind a statement or argument.
- Provide structured reasoning and support for an argument that we wish to make.

It's important to recognize that no one thinks critically all the time, as our thinking can be influenced by emotions or other external factors. However, the ability to think critically can be improved and refined through deliberate practice and the application of specific techniques to different problems.

4. Analytical Thinking:

Analytical thinking involves breaking down complex problems into smaller, manageable parts, examining each of these parts individually, and using this analysis to gain a better understanding of the whole. It is a methodical and systematic approach to solving problems that involves detailed examination and logical reasoning.

Analytical thinking skills allow you to evaluate complex situations or issues and break these down into smaller, more manageable parts that can be analyzed. These parts are then scrutinized to understand patterns, trends, or relationships that can help inform decision-making and problem-solving.

Here are some tips to develop your analytical thinking skills:

- Practice Active Observation:
  Take note of your surroundings, the people, and events happening around you. Careful observation can reveal a lot about how things work and uncover details that might not be apparent at first glance.
- Learn to Ask Questions:
  Cultivate curiosity and don't be afraid to ask questions. Questioning allows you to delve deeper into complex situations and understand the underlying factors that influence outcomes.
- Develop Logical Reasoning:
  Logic is a cornerstone of analytical thinking. Logical reasoning involves examining the elements in a situation, identifying their relationships to each other, and determining how these relationships influence the outcome of the situation.
- Break Down Complex Problems:

One of the key aspects of analytical thinking is being able to dissect a complex problem into smaller, more manageable parts. By understanding each part, you can develop solutions that address the problem.

- Practice Decision-Making:
  Analytical thinking is a key component in effective decision-making. You can practice this by examining various decision scenarios and evaluating the potential outcomes of different courses of action.

Tips:

Analytical thinking and critical thinking are interrelated and often used together in problem-solving. While critical thinking helps to evaluate and scrutinize arguments, analytical thinking assists in dissecting the argument to understand the processes involved. They complement each other to provide a comprehensive approach to problem-solving and decision-making.

5. Concrete Thinking:

Concrete thinking refers to the process of thinking about things that are tangible, physical, and can be perceived through the senses. Concrete thinkers focus on the "here and now", the immediate situation, objects that are physically present, or specific details. This type of thinking is about facts, not theories. It involves thinking in literal terms and being guided by cognitive processes that are based on direct observation and personal experience.

Concrete thinking is often contrasted with abstract thinking. Abstract thinkers can understand and consider complex concepts that can't be physically observed or experienced, such as philosophical ideas or theories. Concrete thinkers, however, may struggle with this because they think in terms of what is tangible and observable.

Here are some examples of concrete thinking:

- If you ask a concrete thinker about a "key", they will likely think about a physical key used to open a door. An abstract thinker, on the other hand, might consider other interpretations, such as a key point in an argument or a key player in a team.

- A concrete thinker might struggle with metaphors and figurative language. If you tell a concrete thinker that "it's raining cats and dogs," they may be confused because they interpret it literally, rather than understanding it's a phrase that means it's raining heavily.

Concrete thinking is particularly prevalent in children, as abstract thinking develops with age. However, adults also engage in concrete thinking, especially in situations that require a focus on real, tangible, and immediate problems or decisions. Concrete thinking is also useful in fields where hands-on, practical skills are required, such as in engineering or craftsmanship.

To enhance your concrete thinking skills, you can:

- Focus on Details:

  Pay close attention to the specific details of a situation or problem. This includes the physical aspects and observable characteristics.

- Develop Sensory Awareness:

  Concrete thinking is deeply linked to our senses. Practice being more mindful and aware of your sensory experiences.

- Practice Hands-On Activities:

  Engaging in practical activities, such as cooking, gardening, or craftwork, can help you develop a more concrete thinking approach.

While concrete thinking is essential, it's also important to balance it with abstract thinking. This balance can allow us to deal with a range of situations effectively, from the tangible and immediate to the conceptual and future oriented.

6. Creative Thinking:

Creative thinking involves the generation of new, innovative ideas and the ability to see things from a novel perspective. It involves going beyond traditional boundaries and venturing into uncharted territories. Creative thinking is often associated with right-brain activity and is critical in fields like art, literature, music, entrepreneurship, and innovation. However, it also plays a significant role in everyday problem-solving and decision-making. Creative thinking allows you to approach problems and situations from different angles. It encourages curiosity, open-mindedness, imagination, and flexibility. So, according to what is said, Creative thinking refers to using abilities and soft skills to come up with new solutions to problems. Creative thinking skills are techniques used to look at the issue from different and creative angles, using the right tools to assess it and develop a plan. The focus on creativity and innovation is important because most problems might require approaches that have never been created or tried before. It is a highly valued skill to have individually and one that businesses should always aspire to have among their ranks. After all, the word creativity means a phenomenon where something new is created. Creative thinking is a skill and, like any other, it needs constant exercise to stay sharp. You need to regularly expose yourself to situations in which a new idea is needed and surround yourself with like-minded people to achieve this goal.

Here are some tips to foster creative thinking:

- Embrace Curiosity: Be open to learning and exploring new ideas. Ask questions and seek out new experiences. The more varied your experiences and knowledge, the richer your creative thinking can become.

- Challenge Assumptions: Do not accept the status quo. Ask "why" and "what if" questions to explore new possibilities and challenge traditional ways of doing things.

- Encourage Divergent Thinking: This means generating many different ideas about a subject and avoiding conventional approaches. Brainstorming is one technique for encouraging divergent thinking.

- Create an Inspirational Environment: Surround yourself with diverse people, ideas, and experiences. An environment that stimulates your senses can foster creativity.

- Take Risks: Don't be afraid of making mistakes or appearing foolish. Often, creative breakthroughs occur when you're willing to take risks and step outside your comfort zone.

- Practice Mindfulness: Mindfulness helps you become more aware of your thoughts, feelings, and surroundings, which can increase your ability to think creatively.

- Foster Intrinsic Motivation: This is motivation that comes from within, driven by personal satisfaction and interest in the task itself, rather than external rewards. People who are intrinsically motivated are more likely to engage in creativity.

- Seek Out New Experiences: Variety and novelty can stimulate your mind and spark creativity.

- Collaborate with Others: Sharing ideas with others can lead to unexpected creative breakthroughs.

Tips:

-Remember, everyone has creative potential, and with practice, you can strengthen your creative thinking skills. Embracing creative thinking can enrich your personal and professional life by allowing you to see opportunities where others see obstacles.

- Whereas creative thinking is divergent, critical thinking is convergent; whereas creative thinking tries to create something new, critical thinking seeks to assess worth or validity in something that exists; whereas creative thinking is carried on by violating accepted principles, critical thinking is carried on by applying accepted principles.

Types of Creative Thinking

The process of creative thinking is manifested in several distinct forms. Here are a few variants of innovative thought that you might encounter.

. Analysis

Before you can truly engage in creative thought about any subject, understanding it is paramount. This necessitates the capability to scrutinize things meticulously to comprehend their essence. Regardless of whether you're perusing a manuscript, a dataset, a teaching blueprint, or a mathematical equation, preliminary analysis is key.

. Open-Mindedness

To think creatively, it is vital to put aside any preconceived notions or prejudices you may hold and perceive things from a fresh perspective. By approaching an issue with an open mind, you avail yourself of the opportunity for inventive thought.

. Problem-Solving

Organizations value creative personnel who can assist them in resolving work-related problems. When confronted with an issue, contemplate potential solutions before seeking assistance. If the involvement of a supervisor is required, propose solutions instead of merely outlining problems.

Problem–solving skills:

What constitutes problem-solving skills? Problem-solving is a multifaceted capability that involves crucial thinking, decision making, ingenuity, and data processing. Proficient problem solvers employ a methodical approach that enables them to deconstruct complex problems into smaller, more controllable components. Skills indicative of robust problem-solving ability encompass listening skills, analytical thinking skills, creative thinking skills, and communication skills. Both during recruitment and assessment, these abilities should be actively sought and fostered. Problem-solving skills are critical in every professional field and at every level. Consequently, efficient problem-solving may also necessitate industry-specific or job-specific technical abilities. For instance, a certified nurse will require active listening and communication skills when dealing with patients but will also need comprehensive technical knowledge pertaining to illnesses and medications. In numerous instances, a nurse will need to discern when to involve a doctor concerning a patient's medical requirements as a component of the solution.

To solve a problem effectively, you will likely use a few different skills.

Here are a few examples of skills you may use when solving a problem:

.. Research to define the problem

Researching is a vital skill in relation to problem-solving. As someone resolving problems, you need to be able to pinpoint the source of the issue and thoroughly understand it. You can start accumulating more information about a problem through brainstorming sessions with other team members, consulting with more seasoned colleagues, or garnering knowledge through online research or educational courses.

.. Analysis

The initial step to address any problem involves analyzing the situation. Your evaluative skills aid in understanding the problems and formulating effective solutions. During research, these skills are essential to distinguish between viable and non-viable solutions.

.. Decision-making

At the end of the day, decisions must be made on how to solve the issues that crop up. With industry experience, you might be able to decide swiftly at times. Solid research and analytical skills can assist those with less experience in their field. There might also be occasions when it's appropriate to take time to devise a solution or escalate the issue to someone more equipped to resolve it.

.. Communication

When identifying potential solutions, you need to know how to articulate the problem to others. It is also important to know which communication channels to use when seeking assistance. Once a solution is found, clear communication aids in minimizing confusion and facilitates the implementation of the solution.

.. Dependability

Dependability is a crucial skill for problem solvers. Addressing problems promptly is essential. Employers greatly appreciate individuals they can trust to identify and implement solutions quickly and efficiently.

-Creative thinking techniques

As you've learned, creative thinking can be stimulated by several widely utilized techniques. These are effective methods that aid in generating new ideas, testing them in novel environments, and utilizing the inputs of others to make these ideas more innovative. Some exemplary creative thinking skills might include "lateral-thinking, visual reading, out-of-the-box thinking, copywriting, artistic creativity, problem-solving, analytical thinking, and divergent thinking".

 Here are some of the best techniques for creative thinking you can employ.

. Brainstorming

This technique can be highly beneficial for small or large problems that necessitate a creative resolution. The primary objective is to assemble a group of individuals and bounce ideas around without hindrance. The central premise of brainstorming is that, by having an overabundance of creative potential solutions, finding a high-quality solution becomes easier. Brainstorming offers several advantages that can help you hone your creative thinking skills. For instance, it doesn't require a rigid structure and is very informal. However, professional guidance can facilitate it. Moreover, the participants don't even need to be present at the same location; a virtual setup or a shared document can be used. For effective brainstorming, all participants must comprehend the problem that requires a creative solution and should be familiar with the brainstorming process. Finally, don't forget to record all the ideas through proper documentation.

. Lateral thinking:

At times, the solution to a problem is not directly in front of it, but beside it. That's the basic concept of lateral thinking, which is an excellent way to exercise your creative soft skills and formulate innovative strategies. Lateral thinking involves searching in less apparent areas and following less evident lines of reasoning. It can be effective if you and your partners try to view things from different perspectives or invert the problem to see it differently.

For example, the direct solution to a decline in online sales might be to increase ads and promotions. However, lateral thinking might lead to alternative strategies, such as using email marketing to reach customers who haven't bought from you in a while.

. Mind mapping

The process of mind mapping aids in connecting ideas that you never thought could be related. As a result, it could help you find suitable solutions while using creative thinking skills. A mind map is a diagram where you input ideas and connect them. It can list possible solutions to a problem, its immediate repercussions, and the best action plan to handle them. Alternatively, your mind map can serve as a means to see the bigger picture in relation to what you are trying to achieve.

Mind mapping can even be done individually. Sometimes, you might already have all the ideas you need but you need to jot them down. Creating a mind map assists in organizing them and naturally reaching conclusions. Also, since a mind map is essentially an infographic, those who were not part of the process can easily comprehend it. Therefore, it serves as a valid piece of documentation.

. Examples of creativity skills:

In addition to the creative thinking techniques mentioned in this section, there are several other skills. Some creativity skills might include:

". Experimentation. Opposing views. Asking questions and communication."

Four Ways to Improve Creative Thinking

. Thinking outside the routine

Innovative thinking is about "venturing beyond the usual". However, setting certain constraints on your problem-solving process can stimulate more free and innovative thinking. For instance, if you're tasked with preparing dinner, you might find yourself resorting to a meal you frequently make. However, if you're asked to prepare a hot dinner using three specific ingredients and two spices, you're more likely to come up with something unique. This approach to thinking can help broaden your perspective.

. Switch up Your Routine

While a fixed routine can boost productivity, it can sometimes stifle creativity. Therefore, consider changing your routine for a single project, a day, or even just an hour. This could involve minor alterations, like changing your workspace, or significant ones, such as modifying your approach towards projects.

Challenging yourself to adapt to something different will help you discover creative strategies to adapt to your new environment.

. Challenge What's Currently Working

Consider how you might enhance or extend a current process. What would your approach be if you had more resources, be it time, money, or additional expertise? Conversely, what if you had fewer resources? What if the project was taking place at a different time of the year? Or if the target audience was different? Envisioning these various potential scenarios will push you to problem-solve and adjust for a range of (very plausible) circumstances.

. Find Inspiration

Innovative thinking doesn't occur in isolation. It's crucial to solicit opinions, ideas, and feedback from others. Creative thinkers value multiple viewpoints and are curious about others' thought processes. Query your colleague about their work methods, whether it's how they conduct research for a client deliverable or how they approach meeting with an external buyer.

7. Abstract Thinking:

Conceptual thinking involves employing symbols and notions to establish links and align ideas with the broader context. This form of thinking enables you to solve riddles, interpret illusions, and discover hidden meanings. This mode of thinking prompts you to seek specific examples. When someone asserts something, you're inclined to seek evidence supporting their claim, scrutinize why the evidence backs their argument, and understand the mechanism of their reasoning.

-Determining Your Thinking Style:

To identify the thinking style you typically employ, consider the following:

. Reflect on Your Problem-Solving Approach:

You likely utilize one (or more) thinking style(s) when confronted with a problem. Reflect on the last issue you resolved and identify whether you opted for unconventional solutions or if you stuck to logical, sequential steps.

. Assess Your Interaction Style with Others:

Your thinking style often manifests through your interactions with others. Contemplate how you engage with colleagues or family members. For instance, if you're deciding on a lunch location with a group and your initial thought is about limitations (dietary restrictions, food preferences, everyone's proximity, etc.) before proposing a place, you may be a convergent thinker.

. Note Your Interests:

Your thinking style might be linked to your interests. For example, if you're fascinated by free-thinking, creative activities (like poetry and art), you might be a creative thinker. If you enjoy challenges like puzzles and word games, you might be a conceptual thinker. Try to identify a link between your interests and your thinking pattern.

- The biases and thinking

A bias refers to a consistent error in decision-making and thought processes. It takes place when individuals process and interpret their surrounding information, affecting their judgments and decisions. Cognitive biases are often mistaken for logical fallacies. Three main categories of bias include "information bias, selection bias, and confounding". Numerous cognitive biases exist, with some being more prevalent than others. Some biases are social, some pertain to memory, while others influence belief formation, decision-making, and behavior. Confirmation bias is one of the most common cognitive biases. It occurs when an individual seeks out and interprets information (news stories, data, or opinions) that reaffirm their preexisting beliefs or hypotheses.

. Signs of bias in a source may include:

.. Strongly opinionated or one-sided perspective.

.. Bases arguments on unsupported or unsubstantiated claims.

.. Selectively presents facts that steer towards a particular outcome.

.. Claims to present facts, but merely offers opinions.

.. Employs extreme or inappropriate language.

✎ Methods of Problem Solving

There are many methods but here I explained the most common ones.

- The term "**Convergent Thinking**" was coined by Joy Paul Guilford, who also introduced the term for the 'opposite' way of thinking, 'divergent thinking'. Convergent thinking refers to the ability to deliver the 'correct' answer to standard questions that do not demand substantial creativity. This is often the kind of thinking required for most school tasks and on standardized multiple-choice tests for intelligence.

Convergent thinking emphasizes finding a single, well-established answer to a problem. It is often used in tandem with divergent thinking in the process of creative problem-solving. When an individual applies convergent thinking, they consciously use standards or probabilities to make judgments. This method of thinking differs from divergent thinking, where judgment is deferred while seeking and accepting many possible solutions.

. **Divergent Thinking** (Creative Thinking or Horizontal Thinking)

Divergent thinking is a thought process or method used to generate creative ideas by exploring multiple potential solutions. It is often used along with its cognitive counterpart, convergent thinking, which follows a set of logical steps to reach one solution, which in some cases is the 'correct' solution.

Unlike convergent thinking, divergent thinking generally happens in a spontaneous, free flowing, 'non-linear' manner. Many ideas are generated in an emergent cognitive fashion. Numerous possible solutions are explored in a short amount of time, and unexpected connections are made. After the process of divergent thinking is completed, the ideas and information are organized and structured using convergent thinking.

. Lateral Thinking (Using both Convergent and Divergent Thinking) (Thinking Outside the Box)

Lateral thinking is a method of solving problems through an indirect and creative approach. It uses reasoning that isn't immediately obvious and involves ideas that may not be attainable through traditional step-by-step logic. The primary purpose of lateral thinking is not to judge the truth value of statements, as in critical thinking, but to explore the "movement value" of ideas. Lateral thinking moves from one known idea to new ideas, enabling innovative problem-solving.

The term "lateral thinking" was introduced by Edward de Bono in his 1967 book "New Think: The Use of Lateral Thinking". According to de Bono, lateral thinking is a deliberate, systematic creative-thinking process that purposefully looks at challenges from entirely different angles. By introducing specific, unconventional thinking techniques, lateral thinking enables thinkers to uncover novel solutions that would otherwise remain undiscovered.

Lateral thinking differs from traditional problem-solving methods as it focuses on what could be rather than what is currently possible.

It centers around four key directives:

- Recognize the Dominant Ideas: This involves identifying the preconceived notions or existing ideas that may be influencing your perception of a problem.

- Search for Different Perspectives: Instead of sticking with a single point of view, lateral thinking encourages you to seek diverse ways of looking at a situation.
- Relax Rigid Control of Thinking: Rather than adhering strictly to logical and linear thinking processes, lateral thinking suggests loosening up and allowing your mind to explore freely.
- Use Chance to Encourage Other Ideas: This encourages spontaneity and open-mindedness in the thinking process, enabling you to stumble upon new ideas or solutions that might not have been considered in a more controlled thinking environment.

Indeed, the techniques or mental tools that you've mentioned can effectively elicit unpredictable ideas, potentially leading to novel and useful solutions for a wide range of problems. Here's a little more detail on each one:

..Alternatives: This technique encourages using existing concepts as stepping stones to breed new ideas. It promotes flexibility in thinking and fosters innovation.

..Focus: This mental tool sharpens or changes your focus to boost your creative efforts. By shifting your focus, you can view the problem from various angles and discover new insights.

..Challenge: This technique encourages breaking free from traditional ways of operating. By questioning the status quo and challenging conventional wisdom, you can uncover new possibilities.

..Random Entry: This tool involves using unrelated or random input to inspire new lines of thinking. It helps break the pattern of logical, linear thinking and encourages out-of-the-box ideas.

..Provocation: This technique starts with a provocative statement or question to trigger innovative ideas. Provocative statements are often absurd, forcing your mind to find sense and potentially valuable ideas in them.

..Harvesting: This tool involves selecting the most promising ideas from the brainstorming session and refining them into practical approaches.

..Treatment of Ideas: This mental tool is all about developing ideas further and shaping them to fit a particular situation or organization.

. Brainstorming

Brainstorming stands as a favored and well-known technique for idea creation within group settings. It has utility across all phases of a comprehensive problem-solving trajectory and is exclusively divergent in nature. The primary goal of a brainstorming gathering is to cultivate an array of unique ideas, free from the constraints of assessment, be it favorable or unfavorable. In pursuit of Quantity Over Quality, all attendees are encouraged to hold back any judgment on the shared concepts, thereby facilitating the unrestricted flow of all manner of disparate, unlinked, and novel ideas. Instead of deriding an idea that may seem out of place, the members of a brainstorming assembly either build upon any proposed idea or continue to conjure up more concepts. Brainstorming sessions, successful in nature, can be spontaneous and casual or they could be meticulously orchestrated and professionally overseen. They can occur anytime and anywhere, be it in physical gatherings or virtual meetups conducted formally or initiated spontaneously over varied telecommunication channels. The sessions can unfold in real-time, with everyone simultaneously working, or they can be asynchronous, wherein participants proffer and swap ideas over time through a suggestion box, regular mail, electronic mail, or any other communication method. A brainstorming endeavor can assimilate any combination of these configurations.

Regardless of the scenario, the outcome of a brainstorming session can be enhanced by articulating a well-defined problem complemented by ample yet not overwhelming background details. Inviting a diverse group of participants capable of offering a wide range of different perspectives can also boost the results.

. Charrette

The term 'charrette' traces its roots to the word 'chariot', echoing the age-old practice of students engaging in last-minute work. This terminology also implies the cart used for ferrying the condemned to the guillotine.

. Today, 'charrette' embodies any collaborative engagement involving designers, especially those final, intense efforts made to wrap up a project nearing its deadline. A formal Charrette setup often comprises creative marathon sessions spanning several days, also known as 'inquiry by design'. Be it an architectural project or any other, an effective Charrette promotes collective ownership of solutions while warding off conflicts. A typical Charrette can be organized in a setting that facilitates day-long work and provides night accommodation. It may be introduced by a public relations endeavor aimed at assembling the right blend of participants. Once gathered, the participants are formally briefed about the issues at hand and the flow of sessions via speeches, workshops, and other means of communication.

Participants are partitioned into smaller groups, where they brainstorm to pinpoint objectives and goals. As solutions start to take shape during the brainstorming session, representatives from the different interest groups are encouraged to interchange ideas, acquaint each other about potential solutions, resources at hand, obstacles and constraints, political dynamics, among other factors.

..**The goal of Charrette** is to wrap up the sessions with a comprehensive implementation strategy along with action plans, which might include models, sketches, reports, and proposals. This could be followed by a report released to the public.

. K-J Method

The K-J Method, conceptualized by Jiro Kawakita in the 1960s, was originally known as the Affinity Diagram. Today, it's recognized as one of the Seven Management and Planning Tools used in Total Quality Control, transforming the basic K-J brainstorming approach into a problem-solving process.

The fundamental cycle involves the following stages:

"Problem recognition, Definition of circumstances, Diagnosis and problem-framing, Solutions and working hypotheses, Solution activation, Programmed solution implementation."

..Preparation:

Prior to the idea-generation session, participants are given a detailed explanation of the challenge, supplied sufficiently beforehand to allow them ample time to generate and anonymously submit their ideas. Subsequently, all the pre-session ideas are replicated and shared among all participants, enabling everyone to contribute more ideas, inspired by the initial batch. All ideas maintain their anonymity. Any feedback regarding the drawbacks of any idea can be anonymously sent back to the idea originators, providing them the opportunity to enhance their original idea or offer alternatives.

..Mind Mapping

Mind mapping is essentially a non-linear form of outlining. The objective is to create a naturally associated diagram of words, concepts, ideas, tasks, decisions, or other data, and to connect individual items based on their associations.

The age-old utility of mind mapping only underscores its effectiveness. Tony Buzan of England is the most recent claimant of the invention of mind mapping, and his name is currently synonymous with this technique.

In present times, visual-thinking techniques closely resembling mind mapping encompass webs, mind webs, webbing, diagramming, spider diagrams, tree diagrams, brain chains and more. Moreover, a consistent influx of mind mapping software keeps emerging, the process is widely taught, and most creative professionals encounter it at some point in their careers.

How to Mind Map:

Mind mapping, at its core, is a non-linear form of outlining. The goal is to construct a naturally linked diagram of words, concepts, ideas, tasks, decisions, or other data, and to connect individual elements based on their associations. Mind maps can be employed to generate ideas, illustrate intricate ideas and relationships, classify related items, and to facilitate one's thought process, studying, writing, and decision-making.

The potency of mind maps resides in their capability to more faithfully represent human thinking. They allow individuals to intuitively arrange elements based on their significance and as they emerge. Items can be classified and grouped instantly and effortlessly. Meanwhile, the person creating the mind map and others can consistently maintain a holistic view of the entire map.

..A very basic outline of how to create and use mind maps follows:

Begin by inscribing or sketching the main idea or the issue under consideration at the center of a writing surface, preferably a large one. As associated ideas come up, represent them at locations around the central idea and link them to it with lines. Persistently add ideas as they come to mind and appropriately connect them to each other.

Morphological Analysis

Morphological Analysis offers a structured approach and format to scrutinize the elements of complex problem situations, aiming to develop innovative solutions by exploring novel combinations.

. Fritz Zwicky, the astrophysicist who unveiled what we now term dark matter, devised his own technique to systematically construct and investigate the multitude of potential relationships in complex problems. Many modern systems that we employ today to identify the most promising new ideas, products, and solutions among an array of possibilities, are based on variations of his method.

.. How to Use Morphological Analysis:

Numerous problems present us with an overwhelming range of potential solutions, yet undiscovered, with only a fraction potentially being new and useful. This method, metaphorically speaking, drains the swamp, by methodically organizing relevant and promising facets of the situation and merging them in a systematic fashion to pinpoint new and suitable combinations. The objective is to dissect the system, product, or process problem into its fundamental parameters or dimensions and arrange them in a multi-dimensional matrix. Then, the aim is to discover new ideas by examining the matrix for creative and beneficial combinations. While some combinations may already exist, others may be impossible or unsuitable. The remaining ones may embody potential new ideas. If you can depict a problem situation in terms of its dimensions or aspects, morphological analysis can reveal unique and often innovative solutions.

...Morphological Analysis Steps:

1. Identify relevant problem attributes. Either an individual problem solver or a facilitated group brainstorms to define problem characteristics, also known as parameters.

2. Make all the suggestions visible to everyone and categorize them in various ways until a consensus is reached regarding the categorizations.

3. Label the groups and minimize them to a manageable quantity. Instead of aiming for a suggested number, take into account the abilities of the group and the time available. Also bear in mind that there are computer applications and other tools that can aid the process. When dealing with the tangible aspects of something like a consumer product, the labels derived from the groupings might encompass parameters such as product components, color, textures, temperature, and flavor as well as package size, shape, function, and graphics. For manufacturing issues, parameters could include material, function, process, construction, maintenance, and so on.

4. The next step involves filling a grid or multiple grids with lists of parameters arranged along the axes. Now, combinations can be identified within the grid. Depending on the number of items involved, a vast number of combinations may be accessible.

5. Exclude combinations that are impossible or undesirable to implement. Set aside those you neither wish to eliminate nor want to implement. Develop as many of the remaining combinations as possible.

Productive Thinking

Hurson's Productive Thinking Model can help you to be more creative when it comes to problem-solving. It's a framework (not a technique) that uses a few other techniques within it such as brainstorming or lateral-thinking and these are applied at different stages of the process.

Productive Thinking serves as a problem-solving and opportunity-identifying framework that is engineered to integrate creativity methods like brainstorming and lateral thinking as required.

. The 6 Steps of Hurson's Productive Thinking Model:

The model has 6 steps or is a 6-step framework to follow. The six steps to Hurson's Productive Thinking Model are:

1- Identifying the Problem to be Tackled

Start by defining the problem. Ask yourself: What is the problem? How did you discover it? When did the problem start, and how long has it been going on? Determine if there is enough data available to contain the problem and prevent it from affecting the next process step. If sufficient data is available, take steps to contain the problem.

2- Defining Success

Visualize an ideal future where your issue has been addressed, and set clear, observable success criteria to appraise potential solutions.

3- What's the Question?

Formulate the challenge as a question. Then brainstorm to generate as many questions as possible. Cluster, amalgamate, and transfer the most stimulating questions into the subsequent step.

4- Formulating Answers

In this step, participants brainstorm solutions, then trim, cluster, combine, clarify, and select one or more for further development.

5- Assess and choose the most promising idea

Evaluate three or four of the most captivating ideas against the success criteria. Select the most promising. After inquiring what is good and bad about each, analyze, enhance, and refine them into a robust solution.

6- Aligning Resources

The final step converts the selected ideas into an action plan with timelines, milestones, responsibilities, and a list of other issues to be resolved later.

-Six Thinking Hats

Edward de Bono's Six Thinking Hats method is a remarkably effective way to debate an issue, resolve a problem or to reach a significant decision. The technique prompts a group to tackle the issue at hand from all conceivable perspectives.

The Six Thinking Hats method defines six modes of thinking, which are designed to be concurrently directed at the problem at hand.

. Benefits of the Six Thinking Hats technique:

As the technique enables an issue or problem to be examined from each perspective in turn, no single view (or person) is allowed to monopolize a meeting or group discussion. Ideas, decisions, and solutions that are reached using the Six Thinking Hats method should, therefore, be more resilient and effective than they might otherwise have been. The technique also motivates participants to tackle any future issues or problems they encounter in a more comprehensive manner. Although most utilized by a group, the Six Thinking Hats technique can also be effectively employed by any individual who desires a well-rounded approach to issues and problems.

.. The Six Thinking Hats technique:

During a meeting, it's common for people to employ varying thinking styles, making it hard to engage in a productive discussion. For example, one person may be proposing a new idea while another is considering the practical aspects of the last suggestion. To solve this issue, de Bono suggests the Six Thinking Hats method where everyone focuses on the same aspect of the problem at the same time by metaphorically wearing different colored hats. Each hat represents a unique type of thought process, as follows:

1). White Hat:

Thought process: Information gathering.

When wearing the white hat, the group focuses on gathering information about the issue at hand. The questions could be about the available information, its implications, the gaps in the information, the additional information needed, and how to obtain it.

-What information do we have about the issue? (e.g. reports, feedback etc.)

-What does it tell us?

- What information do we lack?

- What information would we like to have?

- How are we going to get it?

2). Red Hat:

Thought process: Feelings, intuition, and emotions.

The red hat permits the group to express their feelings and intuitions without needing to provide a rational explanation. It can also be used to consider the feelings and reactions of others, such as customers.

'I've got a hunch that demand for this product is about to fall.' , Red hat thinking can also be used to encourage the group to think how others, e.g. customers, might feel about The course of action."

3). Black Hat:

Thought process: Caution, criticism, and assessing risks.

The black hat is for evaluating the weak points in an idea or solution, determining potential problems, and planning how to overcome them. It's a critical, logical perspective but shouldn't be overused as it can suppress creative ideas.

While the black hat can be the most useful of the six hats, de Bono warns against its overuse, as this can kill creative ideas and positive thinking.

4). Yellow Hat:

Thought process: Benefits and feasibility.

The yellow hat facilitates optimism and positive thinking but with a rational approach. It allows the group to consider the benefits and feasibility of a new idea or decision. Yellow hat thinking is useful in helping a group to see the bright side when they are feeling negative or despondent about an issue, and to view any creative ideas in a rational light.

5). Green Hat:

Thought process: Creativity, new ideas and possibilities.

The green hat is for creativity and innovation, promoting a quest for new approaches and solutions. All ideas, no matter how 'out there', are welcome and should not be critiqued at this stage. Questions to ask can include:

- Is there a new way we could do this?

-What about approaching the issue from the opposite viewpoint?

-Are there any alternatives we haven't yet considered?

6). Blue Hat: Thought Process and Control

The blue hat is typically worn by the facilitator or leader of the meeting. This role involves overseeing the thinking process, ensuring the discussion remains productive, and guiding the group to shift between different hats as needed. The chairperson uses the blue hat to direct the group towards different types of thinking. For example, if the group is running out of ideas, they might suggest returning to creative green hat thinking. They also respond to participants' suggestions to change hats, maintaining the flow and focus of the discussion.

…Putting the technique into practice:

1). Preparation: Before the meeting or discussion, print out the colored hats (which can usually be found in supplementary resources). Attach each of these to a separate sheet of flipchart paper and hang them up around the room. Alternatively, you can ask the group to suggest an issue they'd like to explore during the meeting.

2). Introduction: Begin the session by explaining that the Six Hats technique is designed to encourage everyone to approach a problem or issue from various perspectives.

3). Discussion: Starting with the red hat, ask the group to discuss the issue at hand while 'wearing' each hat in order. Encourage the group to move around the room as they switch between hats. If the group runs out of ideas or the discussion loses momentum, move on to the next hat. If necessary, you can allow the group to switch back and forth between hats, but make sure that each hat is used.

4). Facilitation: You or another group member should take on the role of the blue hat to facilitate the meeting. This ensures that everyone is 'wearing' the same hat at the same time. The person wearing the blue hat should also note down all the group's ideas and thoughts on the corresponding flipchart when 'wearing' each different hat.

5). Conclusion: At the end of your session, agree on actions with the group and assign responsibilities as appropriate. This step will ensure that the ideas generated in the session lead to tangible outcomes. (University of South Hampton,2021)

. SWOT Analysis

The SWOT analysis is renowned as a strategic instrument for business planning, but its value extends beyond that, proving effective for general cognitive exercises too. The acronym SWOT corresponds to: Strengths, Weaknesses, Opportunities, and Threats. By implementing a SWOT analysis, you can enhance your understanding of your organization's internal advantages and challenges (S-W), along with wider external opportunities and threats (O-T). This in-depth comprehension enhances both strategic thinking preparation and decision-making abilities.

- WHEN DO YOU USE SWOT?

The applicability of a SWOT analysis spans multiple stages of a project. It can be used to:

. Explore potential avenues for novel initiatives or solutions to existing issues.

. Take decisions regarding the optimal route for your project. Recognizing your chances of success in the face of potential obstacles can provide clarity in direction and decision-making.

. Identify potential areas of change. If you find yourself at a crossroads, assessing your strengths and weaknesses can highlight key areas of focus and unexplored possibilities.

. Adapt and modify plans during their execution. A new opportunity might broaden your horizons, while a fresh threat could eliminate a previously viable path.

. The SWOT model facilitates a straightforward method of discussing your project or program and serves as an effective tool to structure information gathered from research or surveys.

Systems Thinking

Everything in your surroundings operates as a system, and each system is an integral part of another. By grasping the interconnected nature of the elements around you, you enhance your ability to understand their collective operation, and how these elements can be adjusted, altered, and leveraged to your benefit. This process is known as systems theory. Leadership and management within sprawling complex systems are demanding tasks. The challenges organizations face are so intricate that simplistic solutions often fall short, and decision-makers frequently grapple with numerous conflicting issues and relationships. Systems theory is a problem-solving approach that perceives 'problems' as components of a larger, dynamic system. It involves comprehending how various elements influence one another within a comprehensive whole.

As Albert Einstein articulated, "The problems cannot be solved using the same level of thinking that created them." Systems theory emphasizes the wider ecosystem rather than the problem in isolation. It broadens our thought process and helps us formulate problems in innovative ways. At the same time, the principles of systems theory make us conscious that perfect solutions are elusive; the choices we make will inevitably affect other components of the system. By predicting the consequences of each compromise, we can mitigate its severity or even exploit it for our benefit. Thus, systems theory empowers us to make enlightened choices.

In general, a systems thinking perspective necessitates curiosity, clarity, compassion, choice, and courage. This approach includes the readiness to fully perceive a situation, to acknowledge our interconnectedness, to recognize that problems usually have multiple possible solutions, and to advocate for potentially unpopular interventions. In theory, we are aware of what a system is. In reality, your consciousness currently resides in a vessel that accommodates numerous intricate systems. Yes, your body is a system – a compilation of systems, such as: The immune system, the respiratory system, internal systems, and so on.

Systems thinking is a holistic approach to analysis that concentrates on how a system's constituent parts interrelate and how systems operate over time and within the framework of larger systems. The systems thinking approach contrasts with conventional analysis, which dissects systems into their separate components.

Systems theory can be applied in any research area and has been utilized in the study of business, political, environmental, economic, human resources, and educational systems, among others. Imagine systems theory as a factory. To produce something, the outcome, the factory needs materials to work with, an input.

-Key terms:

Some of the key terms that make up a systems mindset are:

1. Interconnectedness

A shift in mindset from linear to circular is required for systems thinking. The fundamental principle of this shift is that everything is interconnected. In essence, everything depends on something else for survival. Humans require food, air, and water to sustain our bodies, and trees need carbon dioxide and sunlight to thrive. Everything needs something else, often a complex array of other things, to survive.

Inanimate objects are also dependent on other things: a chair requires a tree to provide its wood, and a cell phone needs an electricity distribution network to power it. So, when we say 'everything is interconnected' from a systems thinking perspective, we are defining a fundamental principle of life. From this perspective, we can alter the way we perceive the world, transitioning from a linear, structured "mechanical worldview" to a dynamic, chaotic, interconnected array of relationships and feedback loops.

A systems thinker employs this mindset to navigate and work within the complexity of life on Earth.

2. Synthesis

Typically, synthesis involves combining two or more elements to create something new. In the context of systems thinking, the aim is synthesis, as opposed to analysis, which involves breaking down complexity into manageable components. Analysis aligns with the mechanical and reductionist worldview, where the world is dissected into parts. But all systems are dynamic and often complex; thus, we need a more holistic approach to understanding phenomena. Synthesis involves understanding the whole and the parts simultaneously, along with the relationships and connections that contribute to the dynamics of the whole. Essentially, synthesis is the ability to perceive interconnectedness.

3. Emergence

From a systems perspective, we acknowledge that larger entities emerge from smaller parts: emergence is the natural result of components coming together. In the most abstract sense, emergence illustrates the universal concept of how life emerges from individual biological elements in diverse and unique ways. Emergence is the outcome of the synergies of the parts; it involves non-linearity and self-organization, and the term 'emergence' is often used to describe the result of elements interacting together.

4. Feedback Loops

Given that everything is interconnected, there are continual feedback loops and flows between elements of a system. We can observe, comprehend, and intervene in feedback loops once we understand their type and dynamics.

The two primary types of feedback loops are reinforcing and balancing. Reinforcing feedback loops, which may be counterintuitive, are typically not beneficial. This occurs when elements in a system amplify more of the same, such as exponential population growth or algae blooms in a pond. In reinforcing loops, an abundance of one element can continually enhance itself, often leading to dominance. A balancing feedback loop, however, involves elements within the system achieving equilibrium. Nature has perfected this balance with predator/prey dynamics — but if you remove too many of one animal from an ecosystem, you may trigger a population explosion of another, indicating the other type of feedback.

5. Causality

Understanding feedback loops involves gaining perspective on causality: how one thing leads to another in a dynamic and constantly evolving system (all systems are dynamic and constantly changing in some way; this is the essence of life).

Cause and effect are common concepts in many professions and in life in general — parents' endeavor to impart this type of critical life lesson to their children, and it's likely you can recall a recent instance where you were at the mercy of the impact of an unintentional action.

Causality in systems thinking pertains to deciphering the way things influence each other in a system. Understanding causality paves the way to a deeper perspective on agency, feedback loops, connections, and relationships, which are all integral parts of systems mapping.

6. Systems Mapping

Systems mapping is a vital tool for the systems thinker. There are numerous methods to map, from analog cluster mapping to complex digital feedback analysis. However, the fundamental principles and practices of systems mapping are universal. Identify and map the elements of 'things' within a system to understand how they interconnect, relate, and operate within a complex system. From this understanding, unique insights and discoveries can be used to develop interventions, shifts, or policy decisions that can significantly alter the system in the most effective way. Understanding these six fundamental concepts is crucial for developing a detailed perspective of how the world operates from a systems perspective and will enhance your ability to think divergently and creatively for a positive impact. What stands out as critical for making a positive impact is the ability to develop your own individual and actions.

✎ Steps in the Systems Thinking Method

Start with defining the issue you're attempting to address. Formulate hypotheses to explain this issue and put them to the test with models. It's only after you've gained enough understanding of the situation that you can begin to enact change.

Step 1: To understand a problem by looking deeply at the whole system.

To address a problem, first, understand it. This is done by examining the system as a whole rather than its individual components. Engage with stakeholders to collect their perspectives on the situation. One effective tool for visualizing the organization of knowledge is Concept Maps, which graphically display the system's elements, concept links, proposition statements, cross-links, and examples.

Step 2: Draw Behavior Over Time Graphs

While considering an issue, our perception is typically influenced by the present scenario. However, problems evolve over time, which means they should be tracked accordingly. A Behavior Over Time graph plots a particular behavior (Y) against time (X), assisting in determining the effectiveness of the current solution.

Step 3: Create a Focusing Statement

By now, you should have a clear vision of the problem-solving process. Formulate a statement outlining the team's goal and the potential cause of the issue.

Step 4: Identify the Structure

With a comprehensive understanding of the problem from the statement, the system's structure needs to be articulated, covering the behavior patterns. Understanding these patterns provides further insight into the problem.

Step 5: Going Deeper into the Issues

Having identified the problem and system structure, this step aims to explore the root causes, focusing on four aspects: "the purpose of the system (what we want), the mental models, the large system, and personal role in the situation."

Step 6: Plan an Intervention

Leverage the previously gathered information to initiate the intervention phase. It involves adjusting the problem's related parts and connections to achieve the desired behavior.

Self-efficacy (Self-belief)

Self-efficacy, as articulated by Albert Bandura (1974), is an individual's conviction about their ability to achieve set goals. It is a positive affirmation of one's capabilities and skills, akin to self-confidence. It forms the basis of cultural intelligence. Researchers have extensively studied self-efficacy over the past quarter-century, focusing on the methods leaders can use to foster higher efficacy levels in their team members. Self-efficacy has been linked to improved physical and mental health, learning outcomes, job satisfaction, and family relations. Interventions that boost self-efficacy can enhance collective resilience and capacity.

Individuals with lower self-efficacy may face difficulties during intercultural processes due to a lack of belief in their problem-solving abilities. In contrast, leaders with higher self-efficacy levels confidently overcome obstacles, engage in problem-solving, and devise strategic solutions to challenges. People's self-efficacy beliefs pertain to specific goals and life areas. For instance, if you are confident about excelling in academics due to your skills, you possess high academic self-efficacy.

The relationship between self-efficacy and strategic thinking:

Generally, self-efficacy plays a vital role in developing thinking and strategic thinking as a motivational construct.

 -The benefits of self-efficacy include:

. Resilience to Stress: High self-efficacy levels can aid in reshaping perspectives on stressful situations. Instead of succumbing to self-doubt in tough times, you might be motivated to devise solutions that work for you.

. Increased Motivation: Individuals with high self-efficacy are more likely to set challenging goals and remain committed to achieving them. This determination often leads to greater effort and persistence in the face of obstacles.

. Enhanced Performance: Believing in your abilities can lead to improved performance in various tasks, as confidence often translates into better execution and mastery of skills.

. Better Decision-Making: High self-efficacy can lead to more decisive actions and better problem-solving abilities, as individuals feel more competent in their judgment and choices.

. Improved Mental Health: A strong sense of self-efficacy can contribute to lower levels of anxiety and depression. Believing in your capability to handle challenges can foster a more positive outlook on life.

. Greater Adaptability: People with high self-efficacy are often more adaptable and open to change. They see new situations as opportunities to learn and grow rather than as threats.

. Enhanced Social Relationships: Confidence in one's abilities can lead to better communication and social interactions. High self-efficacy can foster a sense of assertiveness, making it easier to form and maintain healthy relationships.

. Increased Job Satisfaction: In the workplace, self-efficacy can lead to higher job satisfaction and career success. Individuals are more likely to take on leadership roles and pursue professional development opportunities.

1-Who is a deep thinker? and write some ways to be a deep thinker.

2-What other ways do you know to develop thinking skills? Which thinking skills have you used the most?

3-What's the Difference Between Problem-Solving and Decision-Making?

4-Name the characteristics of critical thinking and describe each of them.

5- What's the Difference Between Concrete vs Abstract Thinking?

6- Find out more about the various types of creative thinking, and why having this ability is very beneficial in the workplace.

7-There are a few tools and techniques that you can use to stimulate creative thinking .one of them is brainstorming. Name some of these techniques and describe each one.

8- What are the main benefits of creative thinking?

9- If one of the students doesn't use only the contents of the book to answer the exam questions and gets help from his own mind and analysis. In your opinion, do you think which of the convergent or divergent thoughts he has? Explain?

10-what are the other types of thinking?

11- by studying and examining at least seven definitions of thinking from the view of experts, determine the important keywords of each one and write a new definition of the concept based on the determined keywords and be ready to present it in class.

12- our brains naturally tend to fall into certain shortcuts and tend to stop thinking about things that we do, see, or say regularly." (That is a rule.) On the other hand, "we learn when we have a piece of information and tend to use it again and regularly. for example, it means that we don't have to learn how to use a knife and fork every time we eat.

- According to these two facts, in which direction does a person normally move? And what is the relationship of this person with thinking and creative thinking.

Chapter 2: Strategic Thinking Expressions

Preface:

Cognitive science, strategic thought involves synthesis, divergence, creativity, intuition, and innovation can act as stimulus courses. pursuing innovation and visualizing unique, radically different futures, which could cause a company to rethink its core existence philosophy and its future. Furthermore, strategic thought, characterized by creative, innovative, and unorthodox thinking, can lead to sustainable competitive advantage and a redefinition of the competitive game, fueled by innovative and imaginative competitive strategies (Heracleous, 1998; Liedtka, 1998). So, getting to know this skill and its expressions open a new gate of thinking toward better future.

Definition and characteristics of System Thinking in Comparable with Strategic Thinking

-Comprehension of strategic thought is closely linked with an understanding of the concepts of strategy, system, and systematic thought. As previously discussed, systematic thought is a blend of analysis and synthesis. It focuses on the whole, where the individual parts never overshadow the importance of the whole and should always contribute to the benefit of the whole. Systematic thought influences strategic thought, answering questions such as: How do components function and integrate?

While systematic thought tends to be more synthetic, descriptive, and dynamic, strategic thought is more analytical, decision-centric, and directive. A strategy could be enriched by systematic thought, as it examines each segment of the business (business units or functional areas like IT) in relation to the profitability and long-term viability of the entire organization. Strategic thought involves thinking on a temporal plane; in contrast, systematic thought is about perceiving things from diverse dimensions. Strategic thought is more about making direct decisions to achieve defined outcomes, while systematic thought focuses more on evaluating the system, considering the potential for it to operate differently, understanding the interactions and perspectives with an intention to instigate change more intentionally. It considers the different ways events can propagate through the system and the impacts of an event on various parts of the system. The practice of systematic thought fosters improved strategic awareness; it promotes a comprehensive view of the broader aspects around any problem area (where a problem does not necessarily signify something negative, as there can be beneficial problems as well), and then understanding the consequences of imposing limitations within that area. Strategic thought pertains to the reasons and objectives you want to accomplish in a specific context, and the entire network of interconnected, constantly interacting components and systems.

- Systems Thinking is characterized by openness and dynamism. Systems consist of interconnected and interdependent parts in relationships - if one part undergoes change, other parts within the system must adapt to accommodate this change. Systems stretch across time and space, with changes not being singular events.

- Systems can perform multiple functions, but their ultimate purpose always involves transformation.

- systems thinking holds that everything is either a system itself or a part of a larger system. A system is a set of components which work together for the overall objective of the whole. Broadly speaking, systems thinking is a consciousness of an entire system and the understanding of how modifications to any segment of that system influence other parts and the system. Therefore, systems thinking can be either analytical or synthetic, and it often represents a synthesis of analysis. At an advanced level, strategic thinking concerns your current position, your desired destination, and the strategy to bridge this gap. To function optimally, systems thinking ought to permeate every stage of a strategic process. Strategy cannot exist without an initial understanding of the system, and a system cannot be developed without first establishing a strategy. The crux of systems thinking is to scrutinize and analyze interaction patterns without passing judgment on the interconnected components or systems in a particular context, thereby understanding occurrences in a more objective manner. Strategic thinking focuses on business objectives and the path to achieving them, while systems thinking provides a holistic view of the bigger picture and cause-effect relationships. In conclusion, Strategic thinking concerns your current location, your intended destination, identification of the gap and creation of alternative approaches to predict and provide solutions. On the other hand, systems thinking views the complete picture, the interactions, and relationships holistically and involves the sequential alignment of steps in pre-determined strategic approaches.

While every team in a work or play setting constitutes a system, possibly the largest system is the one we are most familiar with: the natural ecosystem. "Consider the varying interactions of the ecosystem and their evolution," When one element of the ecosystem changes, it triggers a chain reaction throughout the rest of the system, sometimes in unpredictable ways.

-The difference between strategic thinking with systematic thinking lies in their focus areas: "concept" versus "execution."

For instance, strategic thinking can cultivate an exceptional idea or solution for a business, product, or service. On the other hand, systematic thinking aids in establishing the technical procedures required for its actualization. Systems thinkers emphasize that a system is more than just an aggregation of its components; it is the result of the interaction of these parts. For example, if a car is dismantled, it ceases to be a car because it loses its essential functions. An individual employing a system thinking approach would scrutinize individual decisions along with their systematic repercussions.

-Systems thinking suggests that system behavior arises from the effects of reinforcing and balancing processes. A reinforcing process leads to the expansion of certain system components. If reinforcement is not countered by a balancing process, it eventually results in a breakdown. A balancing process strives to maintain stability in a system. Heeding feedback is a critical aspect of systems thinking. For instance, in project management, conventional wisdom might recommend adding workers to a lagging project. However, this tactic might have historically slowed down progress. Paying attention to such pertinent feedback allows management to explore alternative solutions rather than wasting resources on a tactic that has proven to be ineffective.

Methodologies of systems thinking

Systems thinking utilizes computer simulations and various diagrams and charts to model, depict, and forecast system behavior. Some tools used in systems thinking include:

Behavior over time (BOT) graph, which demonstrates the actions of one or more variables over time.

. The causal loop diagram (CLD), which displays the relationships between system elements. The management flight simulator, an interactive program designed to simulate the impact of management decisions.

. The simulation model, which mimics the interaction of system elements over time.

- Systems of Thinking Tools:

A 'RACI 'chart is an excellent tool for systems thinking. 'RACI' stands for:

"Responsible, Accountable, Consulted, Informed".

Considering each of these elements when trying to solve any problem "encourages continuous inquiry into who is accountable for this decision and helps determine who the appropriate individuals are that need to be informed before making a decision or a change," according to Dumeng. For Brown, the iceberg metaphor is a classic tool. "The outcomes we witness are merely what's visible above the water surface," he explained.

When applying the iceberg metaphor to any problem, ask these questions:

. What might be below the surface?

. What are the possible laws, policies, or other pieces of information that affect the problem you're trying to solve?

. What possible issues or concerns might lead to what you see above the water?

Always commence with what you know but employ the iceberg metaphor as a prompt to ask numerous questions about what could be concealed.

Strategy, Strategic and Strategic Thinking Definitions

. **Strategy** is defined by three elements: "ways, means, and ends".

It's essentially the roadmap to reach objectives using available resources to secure a competitive edge. It encompasses the articulation of an entity's mission and long-term goals, as well as the actions and resource allocation necessary for these goals.

. Nature of strategy:

The nature of strategy is the discovery and exploitation of opportunities. The entire emphasis of strategy is on two things: discover opportunities and act on them.

. Strategic:

Relating to the way in which an organization, country, etc. decides what it wants to achieve and plans actions and use of resources over time to do this (Cambridge Business English Dictionary, Cambridge University Press, 2021).

-When we say "To think strategically" means:

In the context of a business, country, etc., 'strategic' pertains to the identification of desired outcomes and the planning of actions and resource utilization over time to realize them (Cambridge Business English Dictionary, Cambridge University Press, 2021). The phrase "thinking strategically" denotes the ability to comprehend the organization's current state, its future trajectory, and the means to that end. It involves foreseeing opportunities and challenges and using that knowledge to steer the organization.

The Meaning of Strategic Thinking

-Strategic Thinking forms the crux of a good strategy. Effective strategic thinking involves connecting dots across four dimensions:

. **Your environment**: It refers to factors beyond your control including environmental, political, societal, market conditions, allies, competitors, and others who can influence your work.

. Your means: These are the behaviors, actions, systems, teams — anything that you can control directly.

. The future: It covers potential opportunities and challenges that may arise due to change or lack thereof. Future changes may bring new possibilities, talent, skills, and resources, but could also introduce threats.

. Your objective: This is the goal or change that you aim to effectuate — whatever your aim might be.

-"Henry Mintzberg" interprets strategic thinking as a comprehensive perspective of business within one's consciousness (Amiran, 2014).

-In the view of "Gary Hamel", it embodies the artful design of strategy, grounded in creative insight and comprehension of business, while "Ralph Stacey" perceives it as blueprinting hinged on learning (Khan Buiki, 2009).

-Strategic thinking serves as a diagnostic and situational examination of the business. It accumulates data and distills it into a layout that facilitates business possibility evaluation. Although not equated to planning, strategic thinking signifies the primary steps towards creating a strategic plan. Engaging in strategic thinking provides value, making it a valuable instrument in assisting management to convert their concepts and ideas into plans.

-Strategic Thinking is a cognitive process that empowers you to steer your organization (or your team, or yourself) towards sustainability and long-term relevance or competitiveness.

-Strategic thinking means setting a target and determining what needs to be established or what steps you need to take to make it a reality.

. Strategic thinking embodies an approach that centers on the three core concepts: "Aim (Customer), Competitor - the obstacle, and Opportunity (potential benefit)."

-Strategic thinking encapsulates the capacity to examine intricate situations, contemplate multiple possible strategies, and design and implement a plan to reach long-term objectives. It necessitates a holistic perspective of the team and its external environment, cognizance of the team's strengths and weaknesses, and the identification of opportunities and threats. It demands a profound comprehension of the market, competition, and trends and the capability to foresee changes and adapt accordingly. It involves creativity in problem-solving, critical thinking, and decision-making skills, and the capacity to interact and cooperate effectively with others and to motivate and inspire teams towards their goals.

-According to Rowe et al. (1986, p. 23), strategic thinking is conceptualizing an organization and deciding on the approach to formulating a strategy that integrates vision, creativity, flexibility, and entrepreneurship.

-Strategic thinking, at its core, is a purposeful and logical thought process that concentrates on analyzing the crucial factors and variables that will shape the long-term success of a business, a team, or an individual.

-Strategic thinking entails the deliberate anticipation of threats and vulnerabilities to counteract, and opportunities to pursue.

-strategic thinking and analysis culminate in a clear set of objectives, plans, and innovative ideas essential for survival and flourishing in a competitive, dynamic environment. This form of thinking needs to account for economic realities, market dynamics, and available resources.

-Strategic thinking demands research, analytical thinking, innovation, problem-solving abilities, communication and leadership skills, and decisiveness.

-Strategic thinking skills constitute any abilities that allow you to utilize critical thinking to resolve complex issues and plan. These skills are crucial to achieving business goals, surmounting obstacles, and addressing challenges.

-Strategic thinking can imply preparing for potential challenges by devising a plan to surmount them if they occur. This can help you anticipate issues and handle them smoothly and efficiently, guiding you towards success through adversity.

-Strategic thinking involves evaluating the environment, pondering "what is happening in the environment and then asking what would happen if …" or scanning the environment, discovering methods to perform more efficiently, being more innovative, and confidently responding to external challenges and opportunities.

- Strategic thinking denotes thinking differently, critically, and logically outside the confines of the box. It's about solving problems in a creative manner and generating innovative solutions divergent from what others have experimented with in the market.

- Strategic thinking unveils a process of conceptualizing an organization and deciding on the approach to formulating a strategy, which comprises vision, creativity, flexibility, and entrepreneurship (Rowe et al. 1986) (Mintzberg, 1994).

- Strategic thinking incorporates five elements: possessing a system perspective, being intent-focused, thinking in time, being hypothesis-driven, and acting in an intelligently opportunistic manner." (Liedtke,1998)

-Strategic thinking involves two distinct thought processes: planning and thinking. Planning concerns analysis, which involves establishing and formalizing systems and procedures, whereas thinking involves synthesis – encouraging intuitive, innovative, and creative thinking at all levels of the organization. Strategic thinking comprises three different processes: collecting information, formulating ideas, and planning actions. (Steptoe-Warre et al. ,2011)

-The main elements of strategic thinking at the individual level consist of having a vision, the ability to analyze, systems thinking, ability to question, creativity, the ability to create synergy, and the ability to establish an advantage.

-In summary:

. Strategic Thinking is a comprehensive cognitive process that involves analyzing and synthesizing information to guide an organization toward long-term success and sustainability. It integrates various perspectives, including creativity, vision, flexibility, and entrepreneurship, and focuses on setting goals, evaluating environments, and identifying opportunities and threats. Strategic thinking combines analytical and innovative approaches to problem-solving, decision-making, and planning, ensuring that ideas and concepts are transformed into actionable strategies. It requires a deep understanding of market dynamics, competition, and trends, and the ability to adapt and anticipate changes. Strategic thinking is essential for maintaining competitiveness and achieving business goals in a dynamic environment.

. The presented definitions lead to the conceptualization of two phenomena: strategic thinking and the strategic thinker. Strategic thinking, as a cognitive concept in strategic management, has practical application in the persona of the strategic thinker, whose common and differentiating attributes impact the organization's strategic behavior.

✎ Who is a Strategic Thinker?

-A strategic thinker is an individual who embraces a strategic viewpoint rather than an operational one, applying an introspective style of thought. Generally, there are two categories of distinguishing characteristics:

. Traits related to the essence of strategic thinking, namely, attitude towards change and tolerance of uncertainty, style of information processing and decision-making, perception of environment, and reliance on empirical data.

. Traits associated with the process of strategic thinking, such as degree of involvement, reliance on purpose, and systematicity of the process.

-The most important manifestations of the strategic perspective are as follows:

. A long-term approach with temporal planning abilities (Hanford, 1995).

. A comprehensive view of the enterprise in its prevailing environment (Kaufmann, 1991).

. Vision and adaptability to change, fostering innovative solutions (Hamel and Prahalad, 1993).

A strategic thinker comprehends the organization's environment and the relationship between the enterprise and its stakeholders. This thinker is a leader in pursuit of novel strategies, superior solutions (Bonn, 2005), innovative strategies, and discoveries to redefine competitive rules (Goldman, 2007). Engaging in the process of creative destruction, a strategic thinker molds the environment in the most beneficial manner using the full capacities of the human brain (Ohmae, 1982).

Reflective thinking style distinguishes strategic thinkers from other leaders, which hinges on:

(1) awareness, insight, and reflection (Dhir et al., 2018)

(2) double-loop learning (Liedtka, 1998).

Strategic thinkers make conscious decisions, reflecting on their prior choices and the reasoning process they employ. In this way, they continuously learn and make purposeful, deliberate, and insightful decisions. Strategic thinkers are aware of their thought process (Casey and Goldman, 2010). Reflection is a disciplined, active pursuit of meaning, leading to a profound understanding of the relationship between experiences and ideas (Dewey, 1933).

 It includes perceiving, criticizing, restructuring, and testing an intuitive comprehension of experienced phenomena, often taking the form of a reflective dialogue with the situation (Schon, 1983).

Hence, the strategic thinker evolves into a "reflective practitioner", applying reflection-in-action (Schon, 1983), transitioning from one experience to another in a continuous, conscious learning process. In this regard, strategic thinkers engage in a process of double-loop learning, questioning existing assumptions and beliefs to generate innovative solutions (Heracleous, 1998). The strategic thinker is a learner, not a knower (Liedtka, 1998). The strategic thinker, i.e., an individual who adopts a strategic perspective and uses a reflective thinking style, is the principal agent of change in an enterprise (Daghir and Zaydi, 2005).

It's the cognitive abilities of the strategist and the motivation to explore new opportunities that provide direction and developmental momentum to the organization. Conversely, numerous industry studies reveal that deficiencies in strategic thinking among top management significantly and adversely impact the company's performance (Mason, 1986; Zabriskie and Huellmantel, 1991; Bonn, 2001).

Tips:

A comprehensive literature review on strategic thinkers concludes that most researchers emphasize common traits distinguishing strategic thinkers from operational managers:

"holistic perspective (Dutta, 2015), systems approach (Palaima and Skaržauskienė, 2010), reflective thinking (Ribeiro, 2011; Dhir,et al., 2018), focus on intent (Liedtka, 1998), and creativity…".

✎ The Structure of Strategic Thinking

Strategic thinking encompasses components such as Investigation, Analytic reasoning, inventiveness, troubleshooting abilities, Interactive and leadership attributes, and a capacity to make prompt decisions.

- What makes a business successful?

The question might seem straightforward at first glance, with 'profit' being the obvious answer. However, for business proprietors and innovators, success might not always be quantified in monetary terms. Financial gains are a result of business success, not its origin. Success in business arises from appropriate investment, talent, strategic planning, diligent efforts, and occasionally, a bit of fortune.

- Buck Lawrimore postulates the 5 Key Success Factors of business, which emerged from the evaluation of over 100 popular books over two decades. As a service provider to its consumers, understanding the needs and values of a business's target demographic is essential to formulate an effective strategy. Recognizing and understanding the five key success factors of business is the optimal method to build foundational knowledge about a company and its clientele. Companies need to enact all five key success factors to attain long-term success. Critical success factors are the achievements that businesses must attain to fulfill their objectives.

-There are five major key success factors, they are:

1)Strategic focus.

This aspect implies that the company's objectives, brand, and actions are all directed towards a specific goal. Long-lasting businesses in competitive markets are the ones whose leaders articulate their values and realistic mission. This factor emphasizes adhering to the primary business objective, ensuring every project contributes towards it. A substantial part of strategic focus ensures that the target chosen is derived from the customer's desires and requirements.

-This refers to the roles of leadership, planning, and management and incorporates these key elements:

. A customer-driven company based on up-to-date surveys from customers.

. The company's core values are seriously taken into consideration by all members.

. Leaders set an example with their commitment to the firm's values.

. Focused on having a competitive and sustainable advantage.

. Purpose-driven goals expressed by an inspiring but realistic vision.

. Tactics, responsibilities, and clear strategy back all goals.

-Strategic Focus Key Success Factor Examples:

. Establishing and sharing core values that align with customers.

. Leaders of the business are devoted to upholding the business's core values.

. The overall company mission is pursued through realistic goal setting.

2)People:

The second determinant of business success is the workforce that constitutes the corporation. The team is what propels its growth, which underscores the importance of employing personnel that are competent, reliable, and passionate about performance. This success factor also pertains to how content a business's employees are in their workplace. As businesses need to empower their employees, they also need to offer them ample opportunities for success. Employee satisfaction boosts productivity and improves employee retention rates. Staff selection should be based on individual strengths, talent, and attitude. Equal opportunities for growth should be provided and commendable performance, whether individual or team-based, should be rewarded.

People Key Success Factor Examples:

-Recruiting the most competent candidates based on their expertise and experience.

-Full comprehension of job responsibilities among the company's employees.

-Providing employees with opportunities to contribute significantly to business decisions.

3)Operations:

The routine and long-term functioning of a business is known as its operations. The specific operations that a business manages vary depending on the industry it belongs to. For instance, jeans manufacturing company's operations likely involve procuring materials, production, and sales. The operational activities of a pediatrician's office would differ significantly. For operations to be fruitful, the functions need to be documented and their efficiency needs to be measurable to ascertain if the processes require adjustment over time. Procedures should be optimized, fine-tuned, and oriented to deliver optimum customer value. They should also be explained lucidly to all responsible personnel, so they comprehend their responsibility to create and sustain that value. Operations Key Success Factors could include:

. Processes focused on providing excellent service to the customer.

. All operation efforts being documented and trackable over time.

. Procedures being continually evaluated to ensure effectiveness.

4)Marketing:

Marketing is the link that connects a company with its consumers. Good marketing incorporates several elements, such as targeting the right audience, building a recognizable brand, and assessing customer satisfaction after purchase.

Marketing draws new customers to your brand through media communication, fostering business growth. Without customers, a business is bound to falter. Marketing includes sales, customer relations, and overall responsiveness. A company should monitor customer values, needs, satisfaction, and feedback. The company's unique brand should be positioned based on sustainable and long-term advantages.

Marketing Key Success Factor Examples:

. Defining a target marketing audience for the business

. Expanding the customer base through media communication and advertisements

. Eagerly receiving customer feedback and using it to improve.

5)Finances:

The final determinant of success, which is often the first one people consider, is finances. A company's finances encompass all its assets, including cash, properties, and materials.

Besides maintaining the company's financial records, this aspect also involves the financial attributes of their products. Pricing significantly influences the customer's perception of the product and its sales success. Financial success factors encompass assets, equipment, and infrastructure. A business should manage its cash flow and ensure profitability through effective financial procedures. Management should have a clear understanding of the financial data they track and maintain competitive pricing to provide the best value to customers.

. Finances Key Success Factor Examples:

. The products are appropriately priced for a profit to be made while still attracting and maintaining customers.

. Keeping track of finances for a better understanding of company health.

. Every employee of the company understands how their actions affect profits and finances.

Creativity

Maslow postulates that the potential for creativity is innate to every individual. Creativity isn't confined to any domain and the outputs of creative endeavors can vary widely, spanning from product development to novel ideas and beyond. The notion of creativity can often seem abstract and ill-defined, it symbolizes audacity, as it often involves venturing into the new, the uncertain, and the unconventional. It entails the ability to generate unique and beneficial ideas by amalgamating pre-existing elements.

The term 'creativity' is frequently equated with the image of an inventor or an invention, which isn't entirely misplaced. However, a mere fraction of this creative process culminates in an invention. Often, it leads to enhancements in pre-existing products in response to increasingly complex needs. As such, the novelty of the products can range from simple to elaborate. Creativity refers to an individual's ability to ideate solutions based on their knowledge base.

"Amabil" posits that creativity comprises three components:

"Skills relevant to the field of activity, creative thinking skills, and intrinsic motivation. All three aspects, particularly internal motivation, are profoundly influenced by the work environment."

. There are many creative process models that we will review some of them:

1)Rossman's model:

Rossman's seven-stage creative process model includes the following steps:

-Observing a need or problem: Recognizing and identifying a need, issue, or problem that requires a solution.

-Analyzing the need: Understanding the nature of the need or problem through thorough analysis.

-Examining all the available information: Gathering and reviewing all relevant information and data related to the need or problem.

-Formulating all specific solutions: Brainstorming and developing various potential solutions to address the need or problem.

-Critically analyzing these solutions according to their advantages and disadvantages: Evaluate each potential solution by considering its pros and cons.

-Generating new ideas: Innovative and creative ideas that may lead to new solutions.

-Examining and testing the solutions and selecting and completing the final output: Testing the potential solutions, selecting the best one, and implementing it to complete the process.

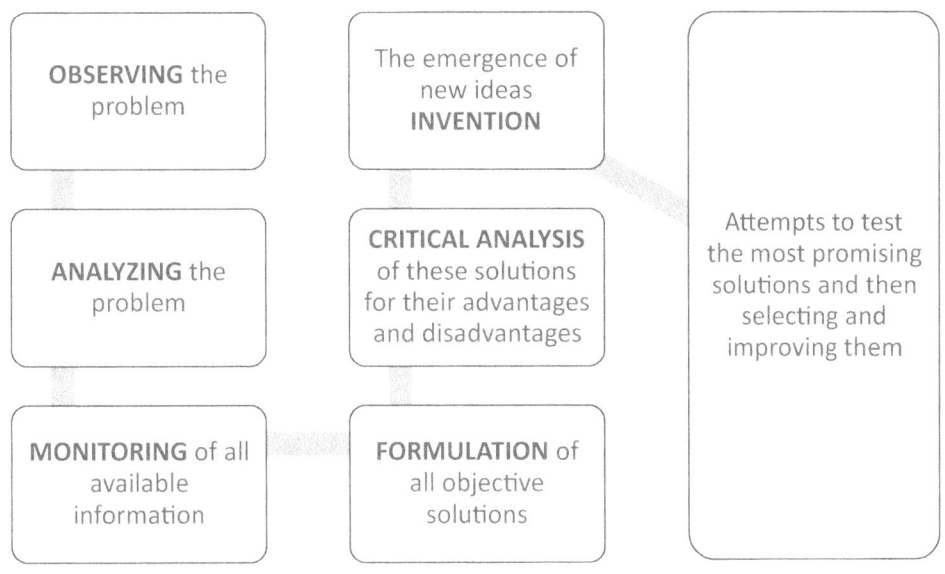

Figure 2.1. Rossman's model

2)Parness model:

Parness offers a six-stage model for the creative process, which includes:

"Objective Finding -Fact Finding   - problem finding - Idea Finding - Solution Finding - Accepting the solution and implementing it."

OF	FF	PF	IF	SF	AF
Objective Finding	Fact Finding	Problem Finding	Idea Finding	Solution Finding	Acceptance Finding
Identify Goal, Wish, Challenge	Gather Data	Clarify the Problem	Generate Ideas	Select & Strengthen Solutions	Plan for Action

Figure 2.2. Parness model

3) Simon model:

Herbert Simon, an influential American political scientist, greatly contributed to administrative theory and was a laureate of the 1978 Nobel Prize in Economic Sciences. Simon emphasized that decision-making is crucial to an organization's functioning, and poor or untimely decisions could impede the organization's goals.

Simon argued that decision-making is a fundamental and crucial aspect of an organization, and any inaccuracies or delays in decision-making can jeopardize the organization's objectives. The process of decision-making encompasses two significant stages: firstly, the act of decision-making itself, and secondly, the implementation of the decision. Both stages carry equal significance.

Herbert Simon was the first to advocate design as a mode of thought and action in scientific disciplines. This perspective was initially proposed in his work, "The Sciences of the Artificial" (1969). Following Simon, numerous design scholars like Robert

McKim, Peter Rowe, Rolf Faste, David Kelley, and Richard Buchanan also championed design as a form of creative, solution-oriented thinking that is applicable across all human endeavors. These scholars primarily approached design from the perspective of the decision-making cycle.

Simon's seven-step design thinking cycle serves as a classic, introductory guideline to an effective design process. This model underscores the integral role of decision-making in creative endeavors and the practical application of design:

. Define

Decide what issue you are trying to resolve, agree on who the audience is, prioritize this project in terms of urgency, determine what will make this project successful, Establish a glossary of terms.

. Review the history of the issue.

Note the existing obstacles, collect examples of other attempts to solve the issue, Note the project supporters, investors, and critics, talk to your end-users for fruitful ideas for later design, consider thought leaders' opinions

. Ideate

Identify the needs and motivations of your end-users, Gen. as many ideas as possible to serve identified needs, record your brainstorming sessions, do not judge or debate ideas, during brainstorming, have one conversation at a time

. Prototype

Combine, expand, and refine ideas, create multiple drafts, get feedback from a diverse group, include end users, present a selection of ideas to the client, Reserve judgement and maintain neutrality, Create, and present actual working prototype(s).

. Choose

Review the objective, set aside emotion and ownership of ideas, avoid consensus thinking, Select the powerful ideas.

. Implement

Make task descriptions, Plan tasks, determine resources, assign tasks, Execute and Deliver to client,

. Learn

Gather feedback from the consumer, determine if the solution met its goals, discuss what could be improved, Measure success and collect data.

4)Amabil Model:

Amabile proposed a five-step model:

"- Presentation of the problem   - Preparation   - Generation of ideas

  - Validation   - Outcome assessment."

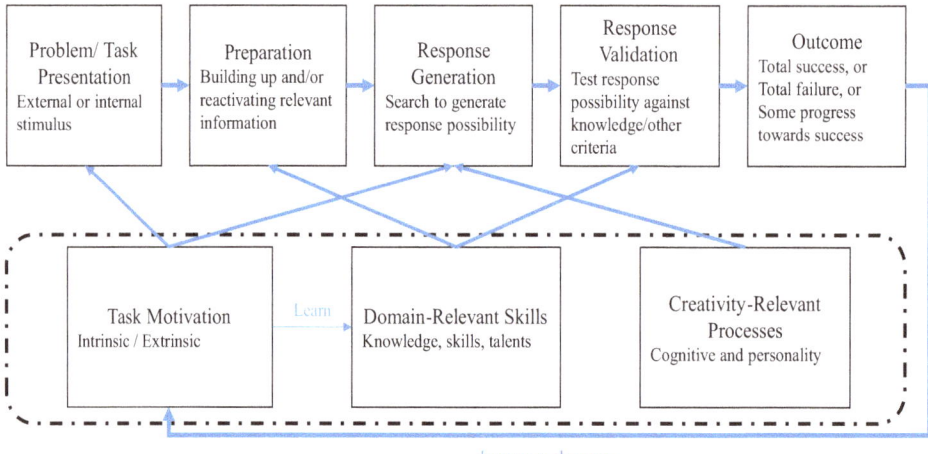

Figure 2.3. Componential framework of creativity

✎ Trend

Starting with the understanding that the universe is in a state of constant flow, one can argue that the future is an extension of the past and the present. Hence, by studying past and present occurrences, processing and analyzing trends that provide a narrative for a series of events, we can make calculated predictions about the future. Trends are indicative of systematic and consistent alterations in data over time. These trends constitute a collection of interconnected events, offering the ability to predict and illustrate potential future scenarios.

Trend identification is a valuable tool for swiftly comprehending and monitoring the external environment. There are numerous factors in the world that remain beyond our control but can still influence our activities. These forces can aid us, hinder us, or act as neutral elements in our operations. The first dimension of strategic thinking - understanding your environment - entails grasping these external forces and comprehending their potential impacts on your endeavors.

In strategic thinking, a standard practice is to examine political, economic, social, and technological trends that are transforming the world around us. This understanding allows us to perceive how the world is evolving, and with this knowledge, we can position our organizations to harness these trends, gaining a strategic advantage that leads to successful policies.

However, the sheer number of existing trends can be overwhelming. The key to understanding trends is recognizing the ones that influence other trends, termed as "drivers". Awareness of these drivers can enable your organization to hold a significant, influential position in crafting solutions that strengthen your community.

Trends can be identified in the short, medium, and long term. Generally, investors hold positions in assets that will remain profitable as long as the current trend persists. Positions that only profit if the trend reverses are considered riskier. Analysts utilize trendlines and channels, essentially boundaries for price fluctuations, to identify and define trends. No trend operates in isolation - they are highly interconnected and interdependent.

A structured trend-mapping process can aid in collaboratively creating important predictions. While no process can entirely predict the future, such exercises are crucial for comprehending the context and anticipating future scenarios. For trend mapping to be impactful, there must be a culture that promotes curiosity, forward-thinking, and risk-taking.

. Trend forecasting in the market:

This involves utilizing market research and consumer data to generate predictions about future customer purchasing behaviors and preferences. Trend forecasting offers insights to product designers that can guide them in designing products that appeal to and are purchased by their target audience.

.. How to find them:

You can find trending topics by browsing social media platforms, industry websites, and forums like Reddit and Quora. However, you'll soon discover that this trend discovery process is time-consuming and inefficient. It might take you hours to discover just one promising trend, and even then, you'll still have to do more research to uncover data to prove it's a trend with promising potential rather than a fad that will disappear in a few months. So instead of showing you various methods to manually dig through data to find trending topics, we'll introduce you to a handful of the most popular trend discovery tools that do the hard work for you. Here's the detailed analysis of the most popular trend discovery tools available which to speed up the trend discovery process:

Exploding Topics, Trend Hunter, Google Trends, Glimpse, TrendWatchers, SparkToro Trending, Trends.co, Buzzsumo,

Awario, Ahrefs Content Explorer, BuzzFeed, Quora, Reddit, Sprout Social, YouTube Trends, Alltop.com, Trendwatching, Pinterest.

Drivers

Drivers are the principal forces of change or displacement that determine patterns and trends in the observable events within our environment and world. They play a crucial role in shaping events and their outcomes in the business environment and throughout a specific timeframe. Drivers can cause events to happen. Every company has its unique drivers, but some common drivers include new product or service launches, fresh financing, resource prices, competitor activities, legislation, regulation, product diversification versus competitors, location, customer satisfaction, cost performance, employee engagement or turnover, profitability, and more. Economic indicators such as inflation rates, interest rates, GDP, and consumer spending can also drive market trends.

Scenario

The shortest and most eloquent definitions of a scenario come from Wendell Bell, who views a scenario as a product of future research methods. He believes that all future research methods serve as a preamble to scenario creation. The scenario method can summarize the results of future research efforts, enabling us to envision possible futures and minimize surprise risks. Each scenario can illustrate a potential future and create an opportunity to scrutinize that possible situation, understanding its opportunities, challenges, and surprising factors. Essentially, a scenario is a glimpse into a future that holds logical consistency within itself.

✎ **Futurology**

Futurology is an exploration of societal, political, and technological advances to comprehend potential future occurrences. (Cambridge University Press, 2023) It represents an intersection of various disciplines that study alterations in the past and present. The examination entails delving into patterns and causative factors of consistency and transition, as well as the origins of such transformations and stabilities. The goal is fostering a future-oriented perspective and charting plausible future scenarios.

The term 'Futurology' was first put forward by Professor Ossip K. Flechtheim (1909 – 1998), a renowned German legal scholar, political scientist, and futurist. He suggested in the 1940s that this term be considered a new branch of knowledge, incorporating an entirely fresh scientific discipline of probability. Futurologists, according to Flechtheim, would strive to scrutinize the premises behind contrasting viewpoints using a foresight methodology.

Futurology as an interdisciplinary study amalgamates and scrutinizes trends to construct probable future scenarios. This process encompasses examining the origins, patterns, and causative factors of change and continuity to cultivate foresight.

Futurology is fundamentally an effort to forecast future events based on available information about the present. It's also known by other names, such as futuring, futures studies, futuristics, and strategic foresight.

The practice is akin to forecasting, which is a tool used by business professionals and economists to predict future trends. However, futurology is more exhaustive and intricate, delving more deeply into the research and offering a more holistic view.

Futurology systematically strives to project future events by analyzing contemporary and historical trends. Futurists employ a variety of methodologies in their work, including the Delphi method and computer modeling. The Delphi technique is a predictive tool involving a group of experts responding to several rounds of questionnaires, with results being shared and discussed after each round, thereby allowing for adjustments in subsequent responses.

. **We can write simply:**

"It is the activity of attempting to predict what will happen based on what is and has happened."

-The characteristics of a good general futurist are:

Develop anticipatory skills and maintain awareness of current and potential changes. Know what to look for and separate important events from noise. Use a macro approach instead of a micro view to data gathering.

The base and essence of strategic thinking is establishing the ability to think strategically. Not everybody, especially early in their career, can't get to participate in strategy formulation, but every single one of us can be a strategic thinker. These three elements are the foundation of competitive advantage: "Capabilities, Activities, and Offerings".

-In your opinion, what do capabilities, activities, and offerings mean and what topics do they include?

1- by studying and examining at least seven definitions of strategy from the experts of Strategic Management science determine the important keywords of each one and write a new definition of the concept of strategy based on the determined keywords and be ready to present it in class.

2- If we want to express a brief but comprehensive definition according to the many definitions that have been raised about strategic thinking. Do you think the following definition is appropriate? If not, what important keywords are not considered in the mentioned definition?

"Strategic thinking is about analyzing opportunities and problems from a broad perspective and understanding the potential impact your actions might have on the future of your organization, or your unit."

3- What is the relationship between creativity and thinking?

4- By examining at least five models of creative process models, while explaining each one according to your desired processes in each of these models, can you present a suitable process model for creativity?

5- What is your idea about the following statement? can you make it complete?

. Strategic Thinking = Systems thinking (holistic /broad /synthetic) + Creativity (reframing /imaginable /non-linear) + Vision (Insightful /directional /temporal).

6- What are critical success factors? Explain them.

7- What are the most important future skills to help you grow your future study?

8- One of the characteristics of a good futurist is:

. Use a radar approach rather than a vacuum cleaner approach to data gathering. (What does it mean? Explain it.)

9- According to the figure below and the information mentioned, and the subjects discussed in the class about strategy, interpret the shape and write a new definition of strategy.

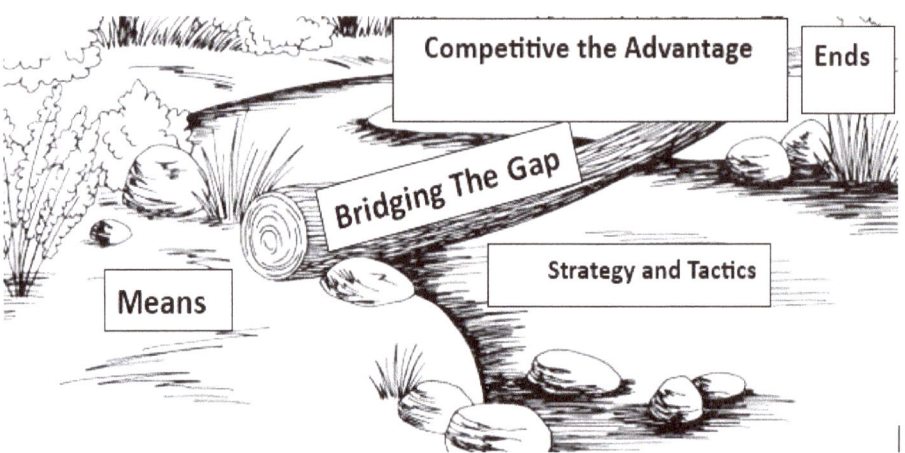

10- Does the figure below show a complete concept of strategic thinking? If not, complete it.

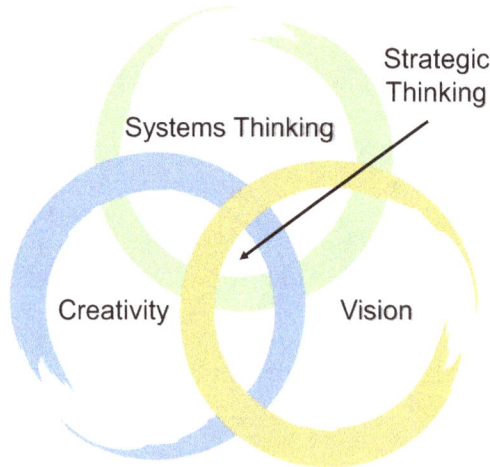

Chapter 3: Strategic thinking

Preface:

Strategic thinking, a cognitive process which likely originated within military organizations several centuries ago, helps in honing the focus on pertinent issues, providing a unified perspective for strategy discussions and reviews. The concept of strategic thinking has been defined in multiple ways, with many leaning towards strategic planning. For clarity, its purpose is better stated as, "Strategic Thinking is a cognitive procedure that empowers one to lead an organization (or a team or oneself) in a manner that ensures goal achievements." It's essentially a way to comprehend effective business drivers and navigate the business towards a superior competitive advantage. It also encompasses the awareness of nascent developments, or those that could potentially occur. Strategic thinking fundamentally involves selecting a long-term goal and devising a plan to achieve it, compelling the thinker to plan several steps ahead. It encapsulates goals, objectives, planning, resources, and more, refusing to be confined to just any single component.

✎ Strategic Thinking Importance

. strategic thinking allows you to formulate your overall goals. It usually precedes strategic planning, as you often need long-term goals before you can develop individual strategies to meet each objective. By continually generating new ideas or potential solutions to common problems, you can practice strategic thinking regularly.

. Strategic thinking allows you to set long-term goals for yourself. A long-term goal can range Are you a strategic thinker? Are you tactical? Does it even matter? Separate studies conducted on leadership published in Wall Street Journal, Chief Executive Magazine, HR Magazine, and the American Management Association all concur that the most valued skill in leaders today is strategic thinking. However, according to data published in the Harvard Business Review, only 23 percent of executives possess strong strategic thinking skills.

. Research by Carroll and Mui further highlights the importance of strategic thinking at an organizational level. Their study of bankruptcies of 750 companies with assets of at least $500 million in the last quarter before bankruptcy from 1981 – 2005 found that nearly 50% of these cases were due to a flawed strategy. In most cases, these avoidable situations stemmed from poorly formulated initial strategies rather than inept execution. If leaders at various organizational levels fail to think strategically today, they might not have business tomorrow. Hence, the ability to think strategically is crucial for both individuals and organizations.

. Today, most managers are expected to deliver more with fewer resources. They have varying degrees of resources (time, talent, and capital) within their organizations. However, not all managers are strategists. The reality is that not all managers are proficient strategists. The more your thinking aligns with strategic thinking and the more strategic insight you possess, the more valuable you become to your organization. The outcome is a high-performance organization where all levels of management are motivated and equipped to mold its strategic direction. Strategic thinking is identified as a business's profound, continuous insights to secure a competitive edge. Consider this, in identical situations, different individuals may react differently.

Some individuals successfully navigate complex problems while others consistently stumble over the same hurdles. Some people build successful businesses starting from scratch, while others overlook such opportunities, deeming them unworthy of their attention. This disparity is because some people can think strategically, while others are not. A person with strategic thinking can think systematically, considering all factors and making calculated decisions.

. The competitive environment can change rapidly for any organization. Emerging trends may necessitate taking advantage of them or risk falling behind. By integrating strategic thinking into your daily work and life routines, you can enhance your skill in anticipating, predicting, and leveraging opportunities.

On an individual level, thinking strategically allows you to make a greater contribution in your role, become more essential to your organization, and prove that you're ready to control greater resources.

. Strategic thinking is the process of visualizing your career goals. It typically enables you to decide what you aim to achieve in your career and how you plan to realize these objectives. You can also apply strategic thinking to improve certain processes, make more informed decisions, or address complex challenges.

. Strategic thinking is a way of thinking or mindset underlying **the strategic management philosophy**.

✎ Strategic Thinking Skills

. At the core of a good strategy is **the skill of strategic thinking**. High-quality strategic thinking involves considering and drawing connections across four dimensions:

Your environment: The world around you that you cannot control, including environmental factors (weather, terrain, etc.), political and societal factors, your marketplace. It also includes allies, competitors, and other types of players with the potential to affect your work.

Your means: Your behaviors, actions, systems, team—anything that is under your direct control.

The future: The opportunities and challenges that you may encounter because of change—or a lack thereof. Everything—your means and your environment—are subject to the future. The future will bring new opportunities, talent, skills, and resources. It could also bring new threats. Skills may deteriorate or become outdated, or resources may diminish.

Your objective: The end outcome or change you seek to create—whatever you ultimately want to achieve.

. Employees capable of thinking critically, logically, and strategically can have a tremendous impact on a business's trajectory. If you want to improve your strategic thinking skills, you can do with the right mindset and practice, in this part, you find beneficial information to improve your strategic thinking skills, so with the study, you can promote your skills.

. You can use strategic thinking skills to achieve business goals and objectives, overcome any challenges and obstacles. These skills will help you to get solutions for problems.

- Key Strategic Thinking Skills:

Strategic thinking skills are abilities that enable you to use critical thinking to solve complex problems and plan. These skills are crucial to achieving business objectives, overcoming obstacles, and addressing challenges—especially those that are projected to require significant time to resolve. Strategic thinking skills include:

1. Analytical skills:

To craft a strategy enabling your organization to meet its goals, the capacity for analyzing a diverse range of inputs is critical. These inputs can range from fiscal reports to market fluctuations, budding business trajectories, and the distribution of internal resources. Your initial dissection of this information is fundamental in formulating a strategy that corresponds to your organization's prevailing circumstances.

2.Communication skills:

The implementation of a strategy in your enterprise, no matter its scale, demands competent communication skills. The facility to express intricate notions, synergize with stakeholders both within and outside the organization, generate agreement, and ensure everyone is oriented and pursuing collective goals are all fundamental to strategic thinking.

3.Problem-solving skills:

Strategic planning is frequently employed to resolve dilemmas or confront challenges such as unachieved financial objectives, ineffective processes, or a burgeoning competitor. Implementing a strategy that targets your key challenge necessitates initially comprehending the issue and its feasible solutions. Subsequently, you can devise a strategy to resolve it.

4. Skills in Planning and Management:

Strategy is not just about ideating a solution—it includes execution as well. Once information has been dissected, the issue has been grasped, and a solution has been pinpointed, you need potent planning and management skills to integrate and align everything.

5.Other skills:

Innovation, Idea generation, Brainstorming, Research capabilities, Leadership, Team collaboration, Futurism,

Comprehension of driving forces, and understanding of different thinking styles are also integral to strategic thinking.

✎ Characteristics of Strategic Thinkers

Strategic thinkers are adept at problem-solving, decision-making, and designing viable action plans to accomplish specific targets. They share certain characteristics:

1. Strategic Foresight: Strategic thinkers possess the skill to anticipate potential obstacles. They are aware that contingency plans can enable quick adjustments when things don't proceed as intended.

2. Curiosity: Strategic thinkers are never hesitant to interrogate or challenge conventional thought processes. They are aware that posing the right query is as crucial as identifying the right solution.

3. Flexibility: Successful strategists can shift when a certain approach isn't producing the anticipated results. They are also adaptable when it comes to reevaluating their own ideas and suppositions when new information surfaces.

4. Pattern Identification: Strategists excel in spotting patterns and extracting meaning from prevalent trends.

5. Ability to Contextualize Information: Strategic thinking necessitates viewing information through the lens of the past, present, and future to cater to both immediate and long-term objectives.

6. Decisiveness: Strategic thinkers are aware that decision-making requires a blend of knowledge and confidence.

7. Market Insight: They grasp their standing in the marketplace, their history, and forthcoming events.

8. Opportunity Identification: They can uncover opportunities and capitalize on them promptly.

9. Innovative Thinking.

10. Alertness and capability in operational evaluation.

Features for strategic thinking

. At least five features for strategic thinking can be counted:

1. Systemic approach: Strategic thinking originates from a systemic mindset. A strategic thinker should establish a comprehensive system of values and comprehend the interconnections between its components.

2. Goal Orientation: Strategic thinking determines the trajectory of the organization and brings it into the limelight. This focal point allows the organization and its members to channel all their efforts in the identified direction.

3. Intellectual opportunism: Identifying opportunities and capitalizing on them is a critical aspect of strategic thinking. This trait implies being open to new developments and experiences and readying the organization to embrace new strategies for upcoming opportunities.

4. Thinking in Time: Strategic thinking is thinking in the organization that links the past, present, and future to each other. Strategy is also a bridge between the present (current situation) and the future. (Ideal situation).

5. In strategic thinking, the future should be created based on today's capabilities (which are the organization's past achievements) and hypothesis driven.

Phases of Strategic Thinking

In simple terms, strategic thinking consists of three phases that identify and clarify:

1) where we are now.

2) where we want to be; and

3) how we will get there.

Figure 3.1. Phases of Strategic Thinking

. Strategic purpose/mission:

Sheila Campbell and Merianne Liteman, in their publication, refer to the strategic purpose as the "core of future plans." It's frequently seen as a lucid understanding of our reason for existence and the significance of that reason. Also termed as a team's fundamental reason for being, when everyone in a team or organization grasps this central reason for existence, numerous daily decisions about tasks become informed and guided by this shared purpose. In the absence of clarity about this shared purpose, priorities are often selected based on personal criteria or in reaction to a crisis.

. Values:

As highlighted by Peter Drucker, "Culture consumes strategy for breakfast." If your culture is ineffective, your strategy will be as well. Values mirror an organization's culture and clarity regarding values allows the organization to leverage them to cultivate a culture that supports its purpose and vision, rather than one that subverts them. Teams can engage in a process that clarifies organizational values and utilize these as the foundation of practices that amplify team interactions and culture.

. Vision:

Vision delineates the trajectory of the activities. It responds to the question, "What would it look like if we consistently fulfilled our purpose with excellence?" Vision creates a compelling depiction of the future of the team or organization. Teams (and team members) function more effectively when they understand where they're headed, propelled by a clear, challenging, and meaningful vision. An effective vision can frame daily tasks and help the team members move cohesively in the same direction.

. Key goals:

"What must we achieve to progress towards the realization of our vision?" Recognizing these priorities that will propel the team forward is a fundamental component of any strategic process. Key goals play the pivotal role of aligning the team's ongoing work with a broader purpose and vision as they help articulate where the team is heading in specific, actionable terms.

. Action planning:

A robust strategy alone doesn't guarantee success—it's the effective execution of this strategy that does. Many times, strategic thinking, and planning processes falter because leaders failed to determine "who would do what by when." Action planning elucidates the ways our daily tasks will help advance the goals.

. Strategic thinking is an essential skill for strategic thinkers. By comprehending components such as the "action plan," conversations can be initiated around pivotal issues and a shared understanding of our identity, destination, and route can be fostered. (University of Florida, 2022)

✎ Five Commands for Strategic Thinking

. First Commandment:

Seek to "learn" from the business environment more than getting information.

. Second Commandment:

Seek to discover non-responded needs more than responding discovered needs.

. The Third Commandment:

Have ultimate goals more than intermediate goals.

. The Fourth Commandment:

Seek to create the capability for competition more than creating the capability for production.

. The Fifth Commandment:

Think about shortcuts in the movement toward the goal more than speed.

✎ Strategic Thinking and its Relationship with Strategic Planning

- Outlined here is a six-phase process that showcases the progression of strategic thinking and the establishment of a strategic planning framework:

(1) Grasp the Present.

(2) Formulate a Vision of the Future.

(3) Pinpoint the Crucial Issues.

(4) Set Objectives and Goals.

(5) Design Action Plans.

(6) Plan and allocate and distribute human and inhuman Resources.

These six phases may vary depending on the strategy. Each individual or business has their unique perspective. Nonetheless, it's a process, formal or informal, that every organization employs to engage in strategy. Strategic thinking emphasizes comprehending the present and determining the critical issues. This is a worthwhile pursuit as it encourages management and business owners to reflect on their enterprise. Often, business owners become too engrossed in day-to-day matters and overlook envisioning the future. Dedicating more time to strategic thinking about the future typically results in enhanced profitability and boosts business value.

-What is the meaning of the following statement?

(Be ready to discuss in class.)

"Strategic thinking is about uncovering all the options and thinking long term."

1- Compare the two issues of "Strategic planning and Strategic thinking" and write down the similarities and differences in comparison of each other.

2-Describe the process of drawing below related to creative thinking.

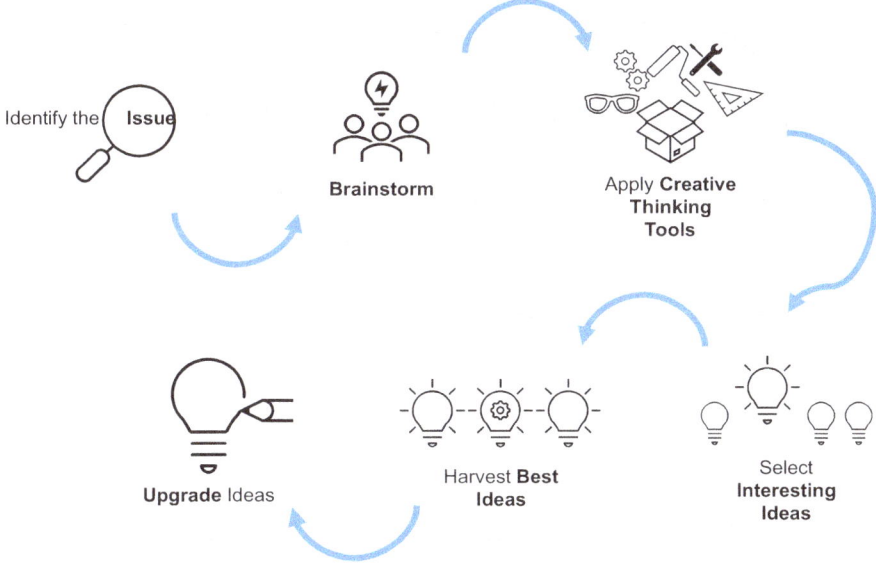

Figure 3. 1. A Process for Creative Thinking

3-Complete the table below by studying the topics of goal and goal setting and the visions of several business companies.

Clear goal	Unclear goal
1-	
2-	
3-	
4-	
5-	
VISION:	
1-	
2-	
3-	
4-	
5-	

-Interpret the figure below.

Strategic Thinking

- External orientation
- Analyze data
- Question assumptions
- Generate new ideas

Strategic planning

- External analysis
- Internal analysis
- Directional analysis

Strategy formulation
- Directional strategies
- Adaptive strategies
- Market entry strategies
- Competitive strategies

Planning the implementation
- Service delivery strategies
- Support strategies
- Action plans

Strategic momentum

- Managerial action
- Strategy evaluation
- Emergent learning
- Re-initiate strategic thinking

Chapter 4: Strategic Analysis

Preface:

The practice of strategic analysis involves studying an organization and the circumstances in which it operates to form a comprehensive strategy. This evaluation process typically includes defining the organization's internal and external contexts, scrutinizing the collected data, and employing various tools for strategic analysis. In today's fast-paced environment, leaders must swiftly comprehend changing scenarios. How can analytical tools assist? They offer a framework that can help streamline and structure your thoughts promptly. These tools, crucial in the business world, can assist in diverse situations ranging from strategic planning, problem solving, to communication planning. They can be used individually, collectively as a team, or at an organization-wide level. They span from abstract frameworks to highly regimented models comprising formal, sequential procedures.

The Key Components in Strategic Analysis

1. Comprehending the Strategy Level for the Analysis

Strategy manifests at different levels, which vary based on your role in the organization and its size. You might be devising a strategy to guide a multifaceted organization or merely framing a strategy for your marketing team. Accordingly, the process will vary for each level due to differing objectives and requirements. The three levels of strategy include:

"Corporate Strategy, Business Strategy, and Functional Strategy."

2. Internal Analysis

An internal analysis is an introspective look at the organization, examining the components that constitute the internal environment. Carrying out an internal analysis enables you to discern the organization's strengths and weaknesses. The insights gained, combined with external analysis, facilitate strategic decision-making for management during the strategy formation process.

The steps in carrying out an internal analysis include:

"Selection of analytical tools. Data collection and research. Information analysis. Dissemination of significant findings."

-The commencement of an internal analysis should be with the choice of a suitable analytical tool or framework. There are numerous tools that can aid in internal analysis. Gap Analysis, Strategy Evaluation, McKinsey 7S Model, and VRIO are all excellent tools that can provide a detailed insight into your internal environment.

-The second step involves research. After selecting the tool(s), the focus shifts to research and data collection. The chosen tool should guide you on what data and information to consider and how to interpret it.

-The third step is the analysis of the information gathered. After the research and data collection phase, it's time to analyze the compiled data and information. How does this data potentially influence your business? Examining different scenarios can help you ascertain potential impacts.

-The last step in an internal analysis is the distribution of conclusions. If the conclusions of an analysis remain unknown, their value diminishes. It's crucial to communicate your findings to the rest of the team involved in the analysis and beyond. Disseminate pertinent information across your organization to demonstrate trust and provide a context for your decisions.

After the internal analysis is concluded, the organization should have a thorough understanding of its areas of excellence, areas of adequacy, and areas with deficiencies and gaps. This analysis equips the management with knowledge of strengths and opportunities, which can be leveraged. It also enables the formation of strategies to mitigate any threats and make up for any identified weaknesses. Starting the strategy formation after this analysis ensures that your strategic plan leverages strengths and opportunities and mitigates or improves weaknesses and threats. You can thus be sure of effectively and efficiently utilizing your resources, time, and focus.

3. External Analysis

An external analysis inspects the environment in which an organization operates and how those elements impact or could potentially impact the organization. A fundamental distinction between external and internal factors is that organizations can influence internal components but have limited control over external ones. They mainly monitor and respond to the environment, rarely altering it.

External factors of an organization encompass the industry in which it competes, the political and legal frameworks within which it operates, and the communities it serves. The steps to conduct an external analysis mirror those of an internal analysis:

"Selection of analytical tools. Data collection and research. Information analysis. Dissemination of significant findings." You might want to employ tools like SWOT analysis, PESTLE analysis, or Porter's 5 Forces to structure your analysis.

4. Share key findings

The importance of clear and frequent communication cannot be overstated. If there's one golden rule of communication, it is this. Acting your findings gives them value. Sharing these findings with your team enables this action. Like strategy, this information is futile if not disseminated across all relevant parties. It's probable that you did not complete the entire analysis single-handedly. Perhaps you led a particular internal analysis project, like a gap analysis, while another team member analyzed the external environment, and yet another completed a value chain analysis. After gathering feedback from all willing contributors, collate all the information and share the comprehensive picture it forms with every relevant person within your organization. While your first step should be to designate a specific location for everyone to access the data, don't stop there. Arrange a meeting to discuss all key findings and ensure that everyone is aligned with the understanding of the organization's environment.

Strategic Analysis Tools

A variety of strategic analysis tools are available, each with its unique applications. Here are some of the most effective tools in strategic analysis:

"Gap Analysis, VRIO Analysis, Four Corners Analysis, Value Chain Analysis, SWOT Analysis, Strategy Evaluation, Porter's 5 Forces, PESTEL Analysis".

Tips: Most analytical tools are built on historical data and past scenarios, and they extrapolate future trends from this data. Therefore, you should always exercise caution when making predictions based on your strategic analysis outcomes.

. Gap Analysis:

Gap Analysis is an excellent internal analysis instrument that helps detect discrepancies in your organization that may be hindering progress towards your objectives and vision. This analysis facilitates the comparison of your organization's current state with its desired future state to identify existing gaps. These gaps then guide the creation of actions to bridge these disparities. The gap analysis is an ideal starting point for structured and meaningful goal setting, focusing on specific process improvements.

.VRIO Analysis:

The VRIO Analysis is a tool for evaluating your organization's resources from within. This analysis aids in identifying organizational resources that could potentially provide sustainable competitive advantages. The VRIO framework guides you in classifying your organization's resources based on their specific characteristics, and it helps you strategize to develop these resources into competitive advantages.

.Four Corners Analysis:

Four Corners Analysis is another internal analysis tool, but it stands out due to its forward-looking approach. While most tools assess the current state, Four Corners Analysis focuses on the organization's future strategy, keeping you ahead of your competitors. This tool helps understand competitors' motivations and their current strategies, facilitating predictive strategic planning.

.Value Chain Analysis

Like VRIO, Value Chain Analysis helps identify and establish a competitive advantage for your organization by examining each business activity to understand its value contribution to the final product or service. The tool emphasizes that each activity should add value to the final product or service, either directly or indirectly.

.Strategy Evaluation

Generally, every company will have a previous strategy that needs to be taken into consideration during a strategic analysis. Unless you're a new start-up, there's likely an existing strategy in place that should be considered during strategic analysis. Strategy Evaluation is a tool to assess previously or currently implemented strategies, pinpointing successes, failures, unnecessary elements, and areas for improvement. This is where a strategy evaluation comes into play. The previous strategy shouldn't be disregarded or abandoned, even if you feel like it wasn't going in the right direction or course of action. Analyzing why a certain direction or course of action was decided upon will inform your choice of direction. A Strategic Evaluation investigates the strategy previously or currently implemented throughout the organization and identifies what went well, what didn't go so well, what should not have been there, and what could be improved upon. This is a very basic description of what's involved in a strategic analysis because we've already written a detailed guide on how to conduct a comprehensive Strategy Evaluation.

.Porter's 5 Forces

Porter's 5 Forces is a valuable tool for external analysis. It provides an overview of your organization's competitive environment, helping to answer critical questions about your industry and competitive position, and aiding in drafting a profitable strategy.

Porter's 5 forces framework performs an external scan and helps you get a picture of the current market your organization is playing in by answering questions such as - why does my industry look the way it does today? What forces beyond competition shape my industry? Where can I find a position amongst my competitors that is profitable? With the answer to the above questions, you'll be able to start drafting a strategy to ensure your organization can find a profitable position in the industry.

.PESTLE analysis:

Pestle Analysis is a tool for examining external factors affecting an organization. It covers political, economic, social, technological, legal, and environmental aspects.

. Political factors – impact of government policies, trading policies or elections.

. Economic factors – impact of economic trends, taxes, or import/export ratios.

. Social factors – impact of demographics, lifestyles, or ethnic issues.

. Technological factors – impact of advancing technology or technology legislation.

. Legal factors – the impact of employment laws or health and safety regulations.

. Environmental factors – the impact of climate change or environmental regulations.

.SWOT analysis:

A SWOT (strengths, weaknesses, opportunities, and threats) is a business management and marketing tool that can be used to scan an organization's internal and external environment. SWOT Analysis is a versatile tool for examining an organization's internal and external environment. It assesses the strengths and weaknesses (SW) within the organization and the opportunities and threats (OT) from the external environment. This analysis tool is an excellent way to engage key stakeholders, especially when team members independently create SWOT matrices and discuss their results in a group brainstorming session.

Figure 4.1. SWOT

. MOST

"MOST" is an acronym standing for Mission, Objectives, Strategy, and Tactics. It is an alignment tool that helps leaders and teams translate grand mission statements into tangible actions or behaviors. With the help of MOST, organizational goals can be refocused and better aligned across different levels. While the tool is profound in its insights, it can also be used for a 'quick study' of any given situation.

. STEEPLE:

"Steeple" is an **external environmental** scanning tool, breaking down into Social, Technological, Economic, Environmental, Political, Legal, and Ethical factors. It assists organizations in understanding external forces that impact them in a structured manner. For instance, the tool helps explore emerging technological trends that may necessitate significant changes in your business model, such as early adoption, alterations in service delivery models, or pricing adjustments.

.5C Analysis

The 5C analysis tool helps businesses evaluate their environment from five different perspectives that can influence marketing decisions:

.. Customers

This is the analysis of the market's total customers that study demographics, psychographics, geography, and other distinguishing characteristics to influence buyers' behavior. All these factors help understand the customer's buying behavior and motivation behind every purchase.

.. Competitors

Competitors are other companies operating in the business market but in the same industry. Compare the markets of different organizations and what makes them better than others. Understanding your competitors' strengths and opportunities will allow you to identify your threats. You can use this information to develop strategies that mitigate external risks and help your business perform better in the market.

.. Company

This involves analyzing the company itself and the product line, organization culture, internal goals, and objectives. The goal here is to assess whether the company can meet the customer's demand.

.. Collaborators

Collaborators are all those entities that help an organization meet its business goals. These include a network of suppliers, distributors, investors, etc.

.. Climate

When studying the business climate, we focus on the external market environment. Macro-environmental factors include the political environment, regulatory environment, and economic environment. Here you can also assess the current trends and cultural movements in the market. Moreover, in today's digital age, studying the climate also refers to understanding the technological environment and how it is impacting your industry.

. Porter's 5 Forces Analysis

The Porter's 5 Forces Analysis tool is used to comprehend the competitive dynamics in your business environment. To visualize these forces, one can refer to a relevant diagram.

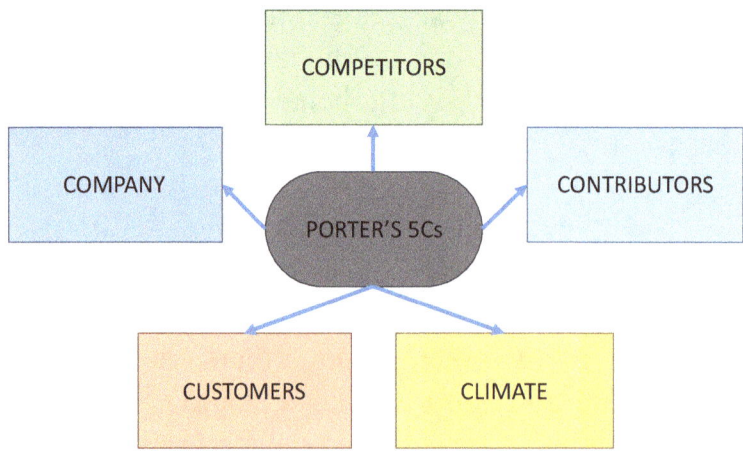

Figure 4.2. Porter's 5 Forces Analysis

1-Describe the following analysis diagram.

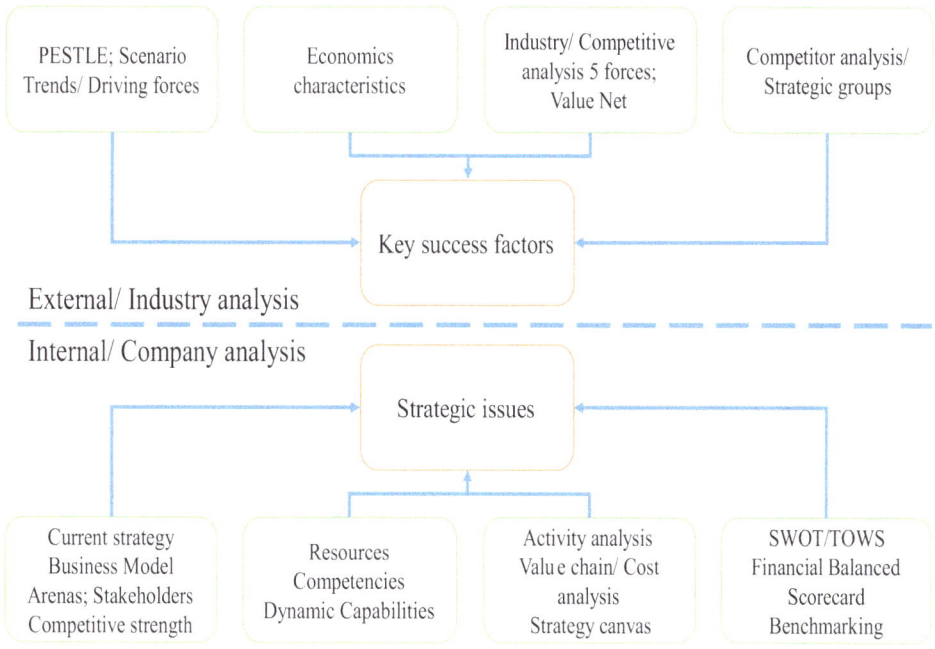

| PESTLE; Scenario Trends/ Driving forces | Economics characteristics | Industry/ Competitive analysis 5 forces; Value Net | Competitor analysis/ Strategic groups |

Key success factors

External/ Industry analysis

Internal/ Company analysis

Strategic issues

| Current strategy Business Model Arenas; Stakeholders Competitive strength | Resources Competencies Dynamic Capabilities | Activity analysis Value chain/ Cost analysis Strategy canvas | SWOT/TOWS Financial Balanced Scorecard Benchmarking |

2-Describe the following picture and statement.

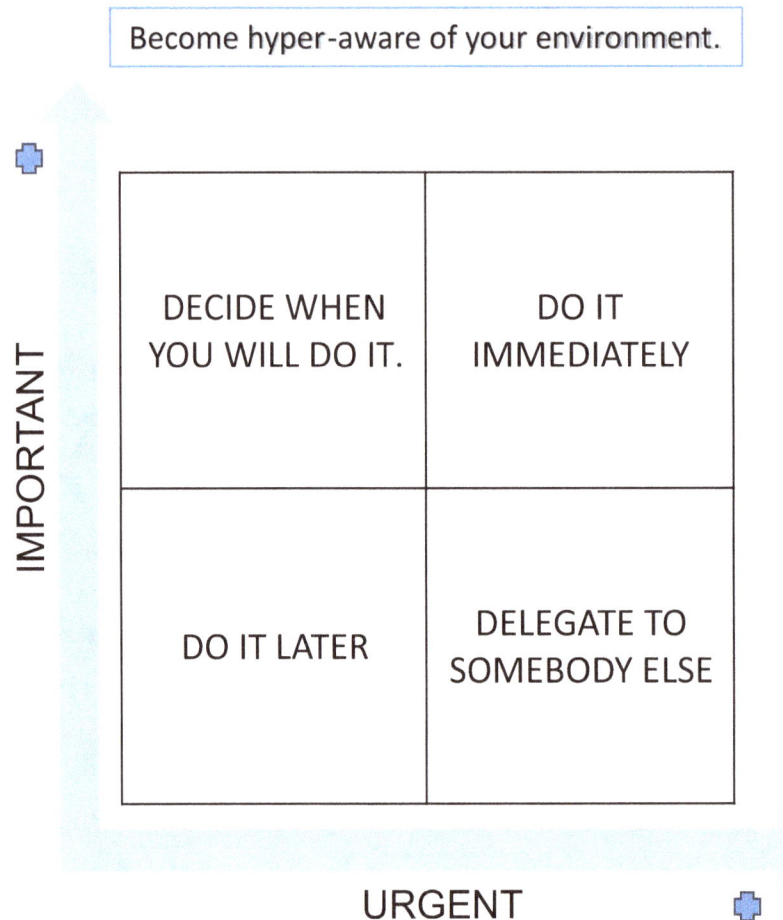

Become hyper-aware of your environment.

IMPORTANT

| DECIDE WHEN YOU WILL DO IT. | DO IT IMMEDIATELY |
| DO IT LATER | DELEGATE TO SOMEBODY ELSE |

URGENT

Chapter 5: How to Improve the Strategic Thinking Skills?

Preface:

The business environment requires rapid-fire decisions from entrepreneurs, managers, and business proprietors. Such decisions ought to be made rationally and with a clear head, considering all viable options. Fine-tuned strategic thinking abilities are vital to the financial success, expansion, and overall prosperity of a company. Investing time in sharpening these skills is worthwhile. A strategic thinker is open-minded and capable of questioning and scrutinizing information. Strategic thinking enhances understanding and tests widely accepted thinking systems, paving the way for originality. People with these traits are indispensable and coveted by progressive employers. Indeed, it ranks highly among the vital skills required to excel in the modern workforce. The development of strategic thinking skills is crucial for personal triumph and societal progression. The most brilliant minds and trailblazers were strategic thinkers who think strategically and explore novel ideas.

✎ How to Improve

-Not everyone has an innate aptitude for strategic thinking, but it can be nurtured. "Regular application and practice of a strategic mindset is what cultivates the ability to think strategically," "Providing opportunities to strategize, even when the outcome may not be successful, is akin to learning to ride a bicycle." Implementing these opportunities and following the tips below will gradually become a habit and fortify our strategic thinking competencies.

-There could be multiple reasons behind your aspiration to become a more strategic thinker—maybe you wish to augment your business acumen, introduce more focus, and purpose in your personal life, or improve your thinking power in game. Regardless of the reason, enhancing your strategic prowess involves contemplating the broader scenario—strategic thinking allows you to envision diverse outcomes, facilitating future planning. It might require some practice and stepping outside your comfort zone, but persistence will result in the gradual improvement of your strategic outlook. Strategic thinking can be improved through the following steps:

1. Ask Strategic Questions:

Scrutinizing established truths and challenging conventional wisdom can help you challenge your prejudices. Questioning your suppositions can also assist you in thinking outside the box to tackle problems.

If you're keen on refining your strategic thinking abilities, one of the simplest strategies is to pose more strategic questions. This practice aids in exercising your planning capabilities, becoming proficient at identifying opportunities, and cultivating a more strategic mindset beneficial for your career. As per the online course by Harvard Business School, strategic questions are pertinent to a challenge, opportunity, or ambiguity you encounter in your current situation, be it personal or professional. They might pertain to the launch of a new business or product, defeating a rival, or structuring your organization for innovation.

Ensure that your queries are relevant to your role and responsibilities so that you can act upon them. Some strategic questions you could ask include:

. How can we strategically position ourselves to enter a new market?

. What's the direction for growth for each of our products or services?

. Where will the organization's growth come from in the next five years, and how does it compare with where growth has historically come from?

. How should the organization respond to the threat presented by potentially disruptive competitors?

2. Observe and Reflect on Your Current Situation:

Besides posing strategic queries, you also need to address them adeptly. One of the most effective methods to achieve this is to observe and reflect on your current situation, ensuring that your strategy is firmly grounded in facts. Suppose your company has started losing market share for one of its products among its traditional customers, but simultaneously, it has gained market share among a completely new customer base. It's easy to make assumptions about the reasons, but doing so could mislead you at a critical juncture in your organization's lifecycle. Instead of blindly following an assumption, gather as much information as possible for use in crafting your strategy. This could include conducting user interviews with new customers to understand the different roles your product fulfills for them. Comprehending why new customers are drawn to your product can help you customize your marketing strategy and product development to better cater to their needs.

3. Consider Different Viewpoints:

After formulating a strategy that can aid your organization in reaching its goals, question your assumptions and put your hypothesis through rigorous testing. This helps ensure that you're not missing an alternative possibility. Planning various scenarios can help you identify potential weaknesses in your argument and prepare you to defend your strategy when others pose questions. It can also sharpen the logical skills required to communicate and implement your strategy. To cultivate this skill, make a habit of questioning yourself whenever you're about to make a statement. Should you consider a different viewpoint? Is there an overlooked alternative?

4. Learn a New Course of Thinking:

While the techniques described above can help you enhance your strategic thinking skills at your own pace, other learning options exist. By learning a new course of thinking, strategic thinking, and innovation, you can learn how to turn innovation into reality for your organization and acquire more skills to identify and implement high-level strategy.

5. Assess What Worked and What didn't.

Post-plan execution, assess what worked and what didn't. What aspects of the process went well that you'd like to replicate next time? What needs improvement? Use all available metrics and any gained insights to refine your next strategic plan.

6. Rank Action Items Based on Importance.

Whether your objectives are personal or professional, ranking action items based on importance can help you maintain focus on a course of action.

7. listen before Acting.

A competent strategic thinker listens before acting. When working in a team, consider everyone's perspective and process multiple viewpoints for a more nuanced approach to problem-solving. When working alone, accumulating as much information as possible can lead to new questions and insights that further refine your strategic plan. (Harvard Business School, 2022).

8. Understand the Strategy-Tactics Distinction

Comprehending the difference between strategy and tactics, and how they cooperate, can assist in building a more strategic mindset.

"Strategy is about doing the right things. Tactics are about the individual actions, complex or simple,". In an organization, it is crucial to do the right things and to do them well collectively.

This can be challenging because people approach strategy differently. Some of your team members may be more strategically inclined, while others may lean more towards tactics.

Consider how we were educated in school, in college, and perhaps in our early professional lives. We were taught to find the correct answer. We were taught to think tactically, trained to perform very specific tasks in the workplace. People are highly focused on the notion of a single correct answer that, if found, would solve everything. Although it's important to ensure your team understands the difference between strategy and tactics, it's also important to understand that your organization needs both strategy and tactics for successful strategy execution. Helping team members understand the difference between strategy and tactics and how they cooperate can help them foster a more strategic mindset.

9. Understand the main three questions: "where we are, where we want to be, and how to get there."

According to Dr. Bock, strategic planning is the process that results in a set of decisions and guidance on future decision-making. Your team members may or may not be directly involved in the strategic planning process, but understanding the process can help them become better strategic thinkers. Encourage your team members to ask three questions as part of strategic thinking:

. Where are we now? Make this an honest appraisal of the situation.

. Where do we want to be? Consider what are attainable goals.

. How will we get there? Identify strategic initiatives and specific tactics to achieve the desired outcomes. The difference between successful entrepreneurs and those who fail is often that the successful ones spend a lot of time thinking and planning before they act.

10. Avoid letting an overflowing agenda hinder your strategic thought process. When situations become chaotic, the instinct is to zoom in on minutiae rather than the broader spectrum. However, strategic insight requires an ability to step away from those granular details. Designate

some periods in your agenda for pure, uninterrupted thought. For instance, if your role involves management, you could reserve a 2-hour slot weekly for high-level strategy contemplation for your division, like mapping out the path for your team and proactive preparation for potential challenges. Keep your focus on overarching plans during this strategic time, jotting down nitty-gritty details for future attention.

11. Detect and address persistent problems. In the quest to understand the larger context, whether it's your entire business operations or the scope of your personal life, observe issues that recur. Identifying these enables easier strategic planning to overcome these hurdles. For example, you might observe that adverse weather in a specific region impacts your company's shipping operations. A contingency plan could then be implemented, like alternative shipping routes or secondary shipping partners. Also, pay attention to repeated strategies in competitive scenarios like chess games. Awareness of the opponent's tendencies can help you outmaneuver them. Once you're aware of that, you may be able to pre-empt that move—like by blocking a certain piece, for example The best way to understand a market that you're trying to enter and the people that are going to use your product is to actually start writing down clear statements of who is going to be using your product and how they should feel when they use it. Use your time and efforts to figure out who already is in this market space and why it is that they won't be able to capture what you will. Look at three or four other players in the market that could potentially disrupt and take advantage of this opportunity in the next year or two and weigh in to see whether you need to enter the market today, wait a couple of years, or maybe not enter it at all.

12. Cultivate curiosity and release preconceived notions. Strategic thinking often involves challenging established norms, therefore, make it a habit to scrutinize your own thoughts. Don't hesitate to question existing practices, or ponder over potential alternatives, and dig deeper when things seem ambiguous or unclear. Adopting this attitude can facilitate innovative problem-solving approaches. Whether it's a messy

office filing system or the potential pitfalls of a new business venture, this attitude can help create innovative solutions.

If you're planning to start your own business, ask yourself questions like "How could this go wrong?" and "What kind of problems should I prepare for?"

13. Solicit diverse opinions. Surrounding yourself with yes-men won't foster growth—construct a team willing to offer honest feedback. When faced with a problem, encourage this team to share their potential solutions. Their input could provide perspectives you wouldn't have considered alone. This doesn't imply surrendering decision-making control but rather, leveraging different viewpoints to foster creative problem-solving. Make sure to connect with people who willingly challenge your thoughts as these differing perspectives are essential for strategic planning. Especially reach out to people who are regularly willing to challenge what you think, like someone who says, "Have you thought about it this way?" Those opposing viewpoints are crucial for strategic planning.

14. Envision an array of probable scenarios. If you're perpetually in a reactive state, maintaining focus on long-term aspirations becomes challenging. A more effective approach is to stay ahead by predicting upcoming changes or possible complications. This forward-thinking attitude aids in devising a well-rounded strategy. Consider a business scenario where you keep yourself updated with emerging technologies to prevent your services from becoming outdated. You then plan to integrate these advancements to secure an edge. While it's not feasible to predict every circumstance in personal or professional life, being generally ready for different situations makes it much easier to adjust when unforeseen events occur.

15. Instead of merely pinpointing what's not working, cultivate the habit of acknowledging what's going well. This perspective simplifies the task of capitalizing on positive occurrences, potentially pre-empting issues before they emerge. When a problem arises, position yourself as the solution finder, not merely the one highlighting the problem. Take

the example of a team consistently lagging deadlines. You could propose strategies to enhance work efficiency, aiding in adhering to the schedule.

16. Adopt a strategic outlook by centering on long-term objectives. Utilize the SMART framework to ensure your goals are feasible. They should be Specific, Measurable, Achievable, Realistic, and Timely. Besides, form an action plan outlining clear steps towards achieving your goals. Say your marketing strategy involves enhancing your social media footprint; your action plan might include steps like determining your target audience, optimizing your pages, adhering to a regular posting schedule, and establishing a consistent "voice" for your brand. Monitor your progress periodically to ensure your plan remains effective. Remain flexible when revising your plans—an essential aspect of maintaining strategic relevance. This doesn't imply controlling every aspect of achieving those goals. In both personal and professional spheres, allowing for some flexibility, provided targets are met in a timely manner, is crucial.

17. Avoid getting sidelined by minor crises. A competent strategist understands that becoming embroiled in lesser issues can deflect you from your ultimate goals. When a situation demands your attention, consider which resolution aligns best with your long-term objectives. This approach aids in decision-making without wasting time on less critical matters. Allow yourself adequate time for critical decisions—patience is a key component of strategic thinking. Suppose you're managing a business with growth objectives. Investing in new manufacturing equipment might be a worthwhile decision if slow production times are hampering customer satisfaction.

18. Direct your efforts towards the areas requiring the most enhancement. Identify your most susceptible area, then devise strategies to fortify it. This principle, called "improving your worst piece" in chess, can be applied universally—from personal management to large-scale corporate administration. Once the issue is resolved, identify the next "worst piece" and address it.

19. Utilize both hemispheres of your brain. Strategic thinking occasionally demands innovative problem-solving. Still, it also requires a practical and logical evaluation of what's achievable and what's not. Strive for a balanced approach, avoiding over-reliance on either aspect. For instance, developing a new product generally begins with a creative solution to a customer's problem. However, logical considerations like cost-efficiency, customer acquisition cost, and manufacturing constraints must also be considered. Don't hesitate to take risks while formulating your strategy!

20. Reflect, don't merely react. In stressful times, we often transition from one situation to another without reflecting on the events. To enhance strategic thinking skills, retrospection is critical to understand the occurrence, the reasons, and preventive measures for the future. If you've invested significant time in a new product that didn't perform well, you might reduce the need for more feedback during the planning phase. This ensures resources are allocated to promising projects. Learning from errors is vital for strategic thinking, helping avoid future obstacles.

21.Enhance your strategic thinking with sports, video games, and chess. If you're looking for less serious ways to practice strategic thinking, consider some of your favorite games! Chess is known for strategic-thinking boosting. Still, other enjoyable methods can be beneficial: real-time strategy video games can help you develop faster decision-making skills, vital in real-world strategy adaptation. Besides numerous physical and mental advantages, playing sports can also enhance your strategic thinking abilities. (Wiki-how, 2023).

✎ How to be seen as a strategic thinker

. Cultivating strategic thinking skills is not the sole prerequisite for career progression. To climb up the professional ladder, it's imperative to showcase these skills. Leaders are interested in your thoughts, and they assess your promotion eligibility based on your readiness to make larger-scale decisions. Reflect on this: "Is my viewpoint understood by others?" If the answer is no, then you need to find a way to bring your perspective to the discussion. It's equally important to show your capability of implementing new ideas.

. Everyone acknowledges the importance of strategic thinking skills development, but many overlook the significance of displaying these skills to superiors and leadership. Demonstrating strategic thinking signals to your superiors that you have the autonomy to make decisions that will future proof the organization. It assures them that your decision-making process is not isolated but considers the impact on other departments and the external world's response.

. Acquiring robust strategic thinking skills necessitates exposure to strategic roles, assimilation of vast information, involvement in a culture of curiosity, and experiences that enable you to recognize patterns and make novel connections. This is the reason high-potential and leadership development programs often involve job rotations, cross-functional projects, and interactions with senior leadership— these activities expedite the cultivation of strategic thinking.

. Conversely, showcasing strategic thinking requires one to simultaneously act as a marketer, a salesperson, and a change catalyst. Proactive and extensive communication about your strategic endeavors, coupled with the bravery to question others and initiate your strategic ideas, makes you noticeable to your boss and colleagues. Demonstrate your ability to kindle innovation and usher in strategic change. Being seen as a strategic thinker also requires showing that you can apply your knowledge to bring new ideas to life. Regardless of your professional level, you can show strategic thinking by undertaking an innovative project that indicates your understanding goes beyond your present function.

✎ Models for Strategic Thinking

Numerous frameworks are available to facilitate your strategic thinking process. The crucial aspect is to reinforce the process, ensure consensus on outcomes and subsequent steps, followed by their execution. Failing to do this may leave you caught in a strategic thinking loop teeming with good ideas but zero implementation. In this section, I will introduce one of the models of strategic thinking for initial understanding. The remaining models along with the practical application of the knowledge acquired from this book will be extensively discussed in the second volume of the strategic thinking book.

-One of them is the System model. Basically, this model views the organization as a System and relies on the concept of Systems Thinking and how Systems work. So here, try to explain it in brief.

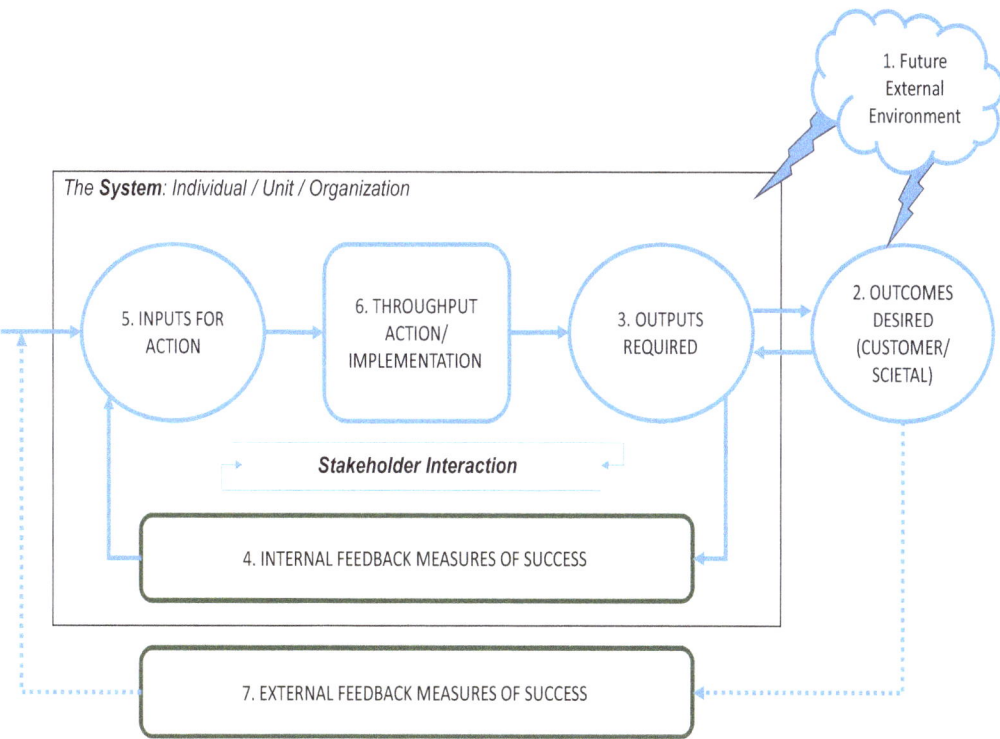

Figure 5.1. System Model for Strategic Thinking

-Step 1: The Future External Environment

The external environment is outside the organization, and therefore outside the control of the organization. In other words, whatever is going to happen in the external environment, will happen whether like it or not. So, to be relevant in its business landscape, a company will need to adapt to the environment, not the other way round. And for the company to remain relevant into the future, it must be able to adapt proactively to its future business landscape. Thus, to understand the External Environment, and how it might change in the Future, is the first and most important step in Strategic Thinking.

-Step 2: Desired Outcomes (Customer and Societal Needs)

Next, the organization needs to decide the impact it wants to have on its customers and society. Such an impact lies in fulfilling what the customers (and society) need to achieve their objectives. This impact, the fulfilling of customer (and social) needs, are necessarily the organization's Desired Outcomes. After all, Peter Drucker said that every organization exists to serve a customer somewhere.

-Step 3: Required Outputs

To achieve the Desired Outcomes of fulfilling customer and societal needs, the organization must produce something - some products and services, benefits to meet those needs. These are the Required Outputs of the organization.

-Step 4: Internal Feedback - Internal Measures of Success

Internal Measures of Success tell the organization when they have successfully produced, or are on the right course to produce, the Required Outputs. They are the quantifiable evidence of the Required Outputs being achieved. You will define what these measures, or evidence, are in this step.

-Step 5: Inputs for Action

This step consists of 3 smaller steps. Firstly, you take stock of the current state, i.e.. where exactly you are now with respect to the

Required Outputs. Then you find out where the gaps are, that you need to bridge, to produce the Required Outputs. Finally, you determine what the organization needs to do, the actions it needs to take, to bridge those gaps and achieve the Required Outputs.

-Step 6: Action and Implementation

In this step, the Inputs for Action are acted upon and implemented. If Steps 4 & 5 are done right, and Step 6 is carried out well, the Required Outputs should be produced and evidenced by the Measures of Success.

-Step 7: External Feedback - External Measures of Success

In the end, whether the customers' (and society's) needs are actually met., the organization has achieved business sustainability. External Measures of Success are the evidence you seek that this is indeed happening. Defining it correctly is paramount. The results will feed into the Inputs for Action, together with the Internal Measures of Success.

-The core of all, these processes are Steps 1, 2, 3. They are where the real thinking takes place. Steps 4 & 7 are the translation of the required outputs and desired outcomes into measurable evidence that you want to see as proof of success. Steps 5 & 6 are essentially planning and implementation respectively.

- In the figure below, the definition of strategic thinking is expressed in three sentences. Can you explain the meaning of sentences with an example?

Strategic thinking is:

THINKING BIG
THINKING DEEP
THINKING IN TIME.

1- Describe the other models of strategic thinking?

2- The conceptual model of strategic thinking is drawn in the figure below. according to what you have learned, articulate the advantages and disadvantages of the model, and if necessary, supplement it by proposing an innovative model.

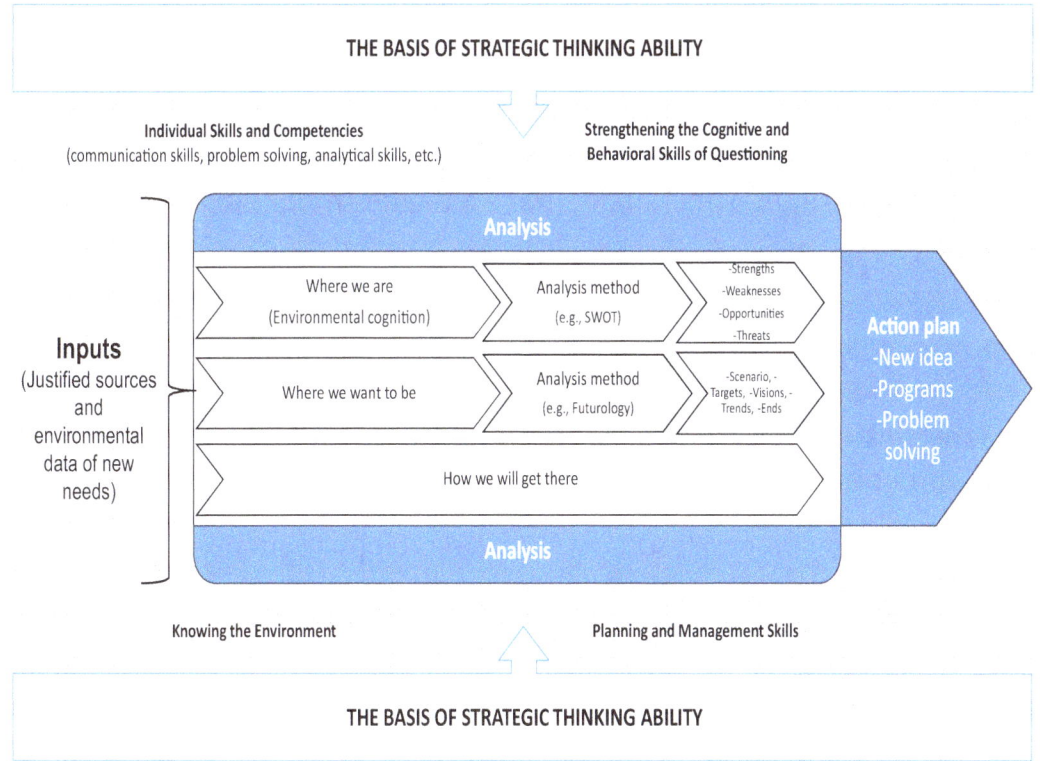

Figure 5.2. Conceptual Model of Strategic Thinking

References:

. Amiran. (2014). Considers strategic thinking as an integrated view of business in the mind.

. Bonn, I. (2005). Improving strategic thinking: A multilevel approach.

. Cambridge Business English Dictionary. (2021). Cambridge University Press.

. Campbell, S., & Liteman, M. (2003). Retreats that work. San Francisco.

. Casey, A., & Goldman, E. (2010). Enhancing the ability to think strategically: A learning model.

.Daghir, M., & Al Zaydi, K. (2005). The strategic thinking skills of Hong Kong school leaders.

. Department of Health and Children. (2001). Primary care: A new direction. DOHC, Dublin.

. Department of Health and Children. (2000, 2001). Annual reports of the Chief Nursing Officer and Chief Medical Officer. DOHC, Dublin.

. Dhir, S., et al. (2018). Defining and developing a scale to measure strategic thinking.

. Goldman, E. (2007). MIT Sloan Management Review.

. Hambrick, D. C. (2007). Upper echelons theory: An update. The Academy of Management Review.

. Hambrick, D. C., & Mason, P. A. (1984). Upper echelons theory.

. Hamel, G., & Prahalad, C. K. (1993). Strategy as stretch and leverage. Harvard Business Review.

. Hanford, P. (1995). Developing director and executive competencies in strategic thinking.

. Hatch, M. J. (2006). Organization theory: Modern, symbolic, and postmodern interpretations.

. Harvard Manage Mentor. (2022). Strategic thinking. Harvard Business Publishing.

. Khan Buiki, R. (2009). Analysis of brokerage office services using the Servqual method. Journal of Business Administration Exploration.

. Kotler, P. (2006). Principles of marketing.

. Liedtka, J. M. (1998). Strategic thinking versus strategic planning. Graetz, F. (2002). Strategic thinking versus strategic planning.

. Nigel, H. (2006). Measurement of customer satisfaction.

. Ohmae, K. (1982). A guide to the strategic planning techniques used by Japanese businesses.

. Ossip K. F. (1998). History and futurology. Cambridge.

. Simerson, B. K., & Olson, A. (2015). Leading with strategic thinking: Four ways effective leaders gain insight, drive change, and get results.

. Steptoe, W., et al. (2011). The importance of the strategic decision-making process towards organizational performance.

. Webster's New World Dictionary. (1988). The word think as the general word .Webster's New World.

Online sources:

. Britannica Dictionary. (2023).https://www.britannica.com/dictionary/thinking

. Collins Dictionary. (2023). Strategic thinking definition. Retrieved from https://www.collinsdictionary.com

. Harvard Business Review. (2016, December). 4 ways to improve your strategic thinking skills. Retrieved from https://hbr.org/2016/12/4-ways-to-improve-your-strategic-thinking-skills

. Harvard Business School Online. (n.d.). How to develop strategic thinking skills. Retrieved from https://online.hbs.edu/blog/post/how-to-develop-strategic-thinking-skills

.Queensland Government. (n.d.). Marketing strategy. Retrieved from https://www.business.qld.gov.au/running-business/marketing-sales/marketing-promotion/strategy

. Strategic Thinking Institute. (2023). How to think strategically. Retrieved from https://www.strategyskills.com

. University of Florida. (2022). Leadership development programs. Retrieved from http://leadership.hr.ufl.edu

. University of South Hampton. (2021). https://www.southampton.ac.uk

. Wilding, M. (2020, June 1). How to be a more strategic thinker. Forbes. Retrieved from https://www.forbes.com/sites/melodywilding/2020/06/01/how-to-be-a-more-strategic-thinker/

. WikiHow Publication .(2023). Enhance your strategic thinking with sports. WikiHow URL

www.ingramcontent.com/pod-product-compliance
Lightning Source LLC
Chambersburg PA
CBHW082135290526
45794CB00008B/3048